Better Homes and Gardens

Celebrate
Volume 2

table *of* contents

salute summer

page 94 There's something about summer that makes everything brighter. Let tranquility and happiness flow with feel-good decorating approaches and party themes that make the most of this warm-weather season.

boo-tify your home

page 116 Brew up a little Halloween magic for your family and friends this year. Fiendish trims, unexpected accents, and tasty treats are yours if you dare. These creative concoctions will please every ghoul and goblin.

easy does it

Make wonderful projects and delicious recipes that take little time yet warrant big applause.

Better Homes and Gardens.

Celebrate

MEREDITH CONSUMER MARKETING
Vice President, Consumer Marketing: Janet Donnelly
Consumer Product Marketing Director: Steve Swanson
Consumer Product Marketing Manager: Wendy Merical
Business Director: Ron Clingman
Senior Production Manager: George Susral

WATERBURY PUBLICATIONS, INC.
Contributing Editors: Sue Banker, Lois White
Contributing Art Director: Cathy Brett
Editorial Director: Lisa Kingsley
Associate Editor: Tricia Laning
Creative Director: Ken Carlson
Associate Design Director: Doug Samuelson
Contributing Copy Editor: Terri Fredrickson
Contributing Proofreaders: Gretchen Kauffman, Peg Smith

BETTER HOMES AND GARDENS® MAGAZINE
Editor in Chief: Gayle Goodson Butler
Art Director: Michael D. Belknap
Deputy Editor, Food and Entertaining: Nancy Wall Hopkins
Senior Food Editor: Richard Swearinger
Associate Food Editor: Erin Simpson
Editorial Assistant: Renee Irey
President: Tom Harty
Vice President, Production: Bruce Heston

MEREDITH CORPORATION
Chairman and Chief Executive Officer: Stephen M. Lacy

In Memoriam: E.T. Meredith III (1933–2003)

Every Day is an Occasion

When I was in college, I worked with an older gentleman who lovingly shared daily words of wisdom. While many have escaped my memory, two witty thoughts remain: "Don't wish your life away" and "If you're breathing, you should be enjoying."

So when I have those "I wish it were Friday" or "Isn't it 5 o'clock YET?" feelings, I think about "Grandpa" Munnings. His words remind me that time IS precious. And while celebrating major holidays is pure bliss, I don't save all the fun and festivity for only those few days of the year.

That is why I stretch. I don't just SEND valentines, I scatter them (decoratively, of course) all over the house so the whole family feels the love (grab some fun ideas on pages 18–21 and 24–25). That's why my porch is decked out for Independence Day the entire month of July (check out the red, white, and blue ideas on pages 108–111). And that's why I make Halloween last for weeks by transforming my yard into a vision that the whole neighborhood enjoys (peek at the cauldron full of yard, indoor décor, and menu ideas starting on page 118).

Besides the holidays, I have a lot of fun surprising my family and friends even when it's simply to celebrate something like the beginning of a new season or a new school year. It's making each day special, in one way or another, that creates those feel-good memories one never forgets.

With that in mind, here's hoping the food, decorating, and party ideas in **Celebrate** inspire you to make every day an occasion for those you love.

Enjoy!

Sue Barker

let the YEAR BEGIN

Start off the year with decorations and celebration ideas that are filled with memory-making magic.

Picture Perfect Birthday

To celebrate a birthday, use photos to honor the celebrator, to surprise the guests, and to wrap gifts with endearing personalization.

Smiling Gift Boxes

■ Replace "to and from" tags with photos that say it all. Wrap papier mâché boxes and lids with wrapping paper or lightweight scrapbook paper. Place a favorite photo in a small metal frame from a scrapbooking store. Glue the frame to the side of the box and place a present inside.

Comfort and Joy

■ Reserve the birthday boy's (or girl's) party chair with an adorable picture pillow.

What You'll Need...

- [ ] premade toss pillow
- [ ] cotton fabrics that complement pillow fabric
- [ ] scissors
- [ ] photo scanner
- [ ] photo
- [ ] T-shirt transfer paper
- [ ] iron
- [ ] fusible web
- [ ] fabric glue
- [ ] decorative trim to coordinate with cotton fabrics

1 Using the photo, opposite, as a guide, cut a square of cotton fabric smaller than the pillow front.

2 Scan a photo with about a 1-inch border on all sides. Print it onto T-shirt transfer paper, trim closely around the photo, and iron onto white cotton fabric (do not remove the paper yet).

3 Iron the white fabric to fusible web. Trim around the photo; remove the backing from the fusible web and iron it onto the center of the color fabric. Press and remove the paper from the iron-on transfer.

4 Use fabric glue to frame the photo with decorative trim and to attach the fabric square to the pillow.

Flower Favors

■ Let guests get into the act with cheery take-home paperweights. To complete the favors on party day, snap photos of kids during the party then print out. Let each kid trim out his or her face and use a glue stick to adhere it in the center of a flower paper cut to fit the paperweight. Sandwich the photos between the acrylic halves of a paperweight.

Seen and Heard

■ It's a picture frame and custom music mix in one. Cut a piece of decorative card stock the width of the CD case and twice its length; fold in half. On the front, attach a favorite photo layered on one or two paper mats. Slip the photo card into the front of the CD case with the fold on the outside. Use the back flap to hold the case open as a frame.

Big Game Bling

Whether you're cheering on your favorite college, high school, NFL team or the boys in the backyard, these football bash ideas are true winners. Get the party started by showcasing team colors, enhanced with glistening gems, small to jumbo in size.

Big Score, Small Budget

■ Using plastic dishes makes it easy to find just-right colors for any sports party. Pennants, made from paper triangles (see patterns on page 155), chenille stems, and sticker letters bring home the theme. Gem paperweights add bling to the bash.

Good Play

■ Gem brads add a touch of class to napkin points while chenille stems threaded with a jewelry disk and button make a napkin ring with one quick twist of the ends.

Two-Minute Drill

■ Just a couple minutes is all it takes to whip together gem-studded woven place mats and favor holders. To trim mats, thread prongs of gem brads through jewelry disks; secure on mat back. For holders, line clean aerosol caps with metallic cupcake liners. Dress up the fronts with press-on gem stickers.

Cozy Comforts

Soft, cuddly flannel is a natural for cold-weather months, but no one would guess that these classy projects are crafted from recycled clothing. Look for flannel shirts, skirts, pajamas, or any clothing that's in good shape. Mix and match plaids, using coordinating colors to unite the look.

Skirt Meets Shirt

A pleated flannel skirt makes the perfect ruffled edging for a soft table mat. Cut a rectangle from the back of a flannel shirt. Hand-tack a strip of the skirt edge to each end. Cover the seam with a contrasting strip of flannel that has the edges turned under. Use embroidery floss stitches like those on page 155 to sew the strip in place as well as to turn under all the raw edges.

Posy-Laden Plaid

■ The key to this clever pillow is a machine-embroidered shirt yoke turned vertically to create detail. To make the cover, measure pillow form and cut a front and back piece 1 inch larger on all sides. With right sides facing, machine-stitch around three edges using ³/₄-inch seams. Clip corners; turn. Insert pillow form; hand-stitch opening closed. Cover a button form with a stitched detail; sew in pillow center using a long needle; knot on back.

Wine Wraps

■ Who needs a wine decanter when you have pretty plaid flannel wraps? These bottle sleeves are just that—sections of shirt sleeves. Cut pieces the desired lengths, turning under the ends slightly. Using a needle and embroidery thread, tack the edges in place using blanket stitches or blind stitches. If desired, trim the wraps with more stitches and buttons.

Coffee Coasters

■ Preserve the table with soft stitched coasters. Cut two 7-inch squares of gingham flannel. With edges aligned, make random cross-stitches on white squares using a variety of embroidery flosses. When the center is stitched, roll over one edge to the front, hiding the raw edges; stitch in place. Repeat with the opposite side, then the remaining sides.

Lovely Liner

■ Fray the edges of a flannel square for simple finishing. To create a focal point, cut a machine-stitched square of flannel, turn under edges, and hand-stitch in place.

Clever Cuffs

■ Transform shirt cuffs into napkin rings. Cut cuffs from sleeves; trim loose threads. Determine ring size; trim off excess fabric from one end, allowing cuff ends to overlap 1 inch. Use cuff button or choose an ornate one. Sew button in place, sewing through both layers. Embellish around button with embroidery stitches as shown on page 155.

My Vintage Valentine

Cute and colorful, valentines from days gone by are found easily at antiques stores and flea markets. Use these affordable little art pieces to add a touch of nostalgia to the special day in February that's dedicated to love.

Heartfelt Messages

■ Choose a special valentine to grace each family member's place at the table. With a red charger base, layer on a large white paper doily, the card, and a clear glass plate. This quick, thoughtful touch will be remembered for many Valentine's Days to come.

It's a Wrap

■ Create old-fashioned wrapping paper by photocopying randomly placed valentines onto white paper. For large packages, wrap the gift in solid red paper first and cut photocopies into strips to act as ribbon, piecing as needed.

Candy Box Buddies

■ Make a heart-shape box of candy an unforgettable gift. Trace around the lid on red paper and cut out with decorative-edge scissors. Use double-stick tape to attach it to the lid. Adhere a heart-shape doily to lid with a glue stick. Tie a bow using black and white ribbons; hot-glue in place. Add valentines under and on top of the bow.

To my Love

Message Bouquet

■ Invite an endearing message to be the center attraction of your Valentine's Day floral arrangement. Tape a card to the end of a skewer and poke it into the center of the bouquet.

Garland of Love

■ Dress up banisters, cupboards, and windows with garlands made from colorful valentines. Choose a large bold card for the center. Then have fun finding cards that face toward center to reinforce the focal point. To turn into a garland, simply string narrow ribbon through ≠cutouts, adding hole punches or slits where needed.

Sweet Greeting

■ Give your sweetie a card bursting with character, literally! Because most vintage valentines have a die-cut shape, they create big impact popping through the window of a blank photo card. Use double-stick tape to hold the card in place as well as a checked ribbon below the cutout window.

Stick to It

■ Make a lucky bouquet to display all month long. Use pretty green scrapbook papers in solids and patterns to trim up bare branches in a jiffy. Cut the paper into squares ranging from 1 to 5 inches; fold in half twice. Trace the patterns on page 154 onto the folded papers; cut out the clover shapes. Unfold without smoothing and hot-glue the shamrocks to twigs, leaving the base of the twigs uncovered. Arrange the twigs in a vase.

Luck of the Irish

Honor St. Patty's Day with shamrocks to admire and to eat, all in tones of earthy green.

Sugar Patty

◾ Add a touch of green food coloring to make sugar cookies a St. Patrick's Day treat. Mix a drop or two into the dough and cut into shamrock shapes. To make double-deckers, spread frosting on a cookie and sandwich with another cookie. Serve warm with a glass of green-tinted milk.

Heart Strings ▶

Using cookie cutters for patterns, these layered hearts connect with satin ribbon to make a touching Valentine's Day garland. Choose solid and patterned papers in red to emphasize the colors of the holiday.

Easy Does It
Objects of Affection

◀ **Sweet Endings**

A brown paper lunch turns into a holiday feast with the addition of beloved chocolate. Use a glue stick to adhere a paper strip to contrasting paper; trim away paper excess using decorative-edge scissors. Write Xs and Os around the edges of the top paper using marking pen. Use double-sided tape to adhere wrapped chocolate hearts to paper strip and clip onto bag with a clothespin.

▼ Sweet Somethings

An arrangement of lollipop flowers with paper petals makes an eye-catching centerpiece. For each flower, fold colored card stock in half and cut out six 2-inch-high hearts. Punch a small hole near each tip. Insert a lollipop stick and arrange six hearts on stem, fanning out petals around the stick.

▲ Heart Felt

The gift of books is made extra special with a handmade bookmark. To make the red-backed bookmark, cut a rectangle out of cream-color wool felt and trace a heart on the back side; cut out the shape with scissors. Glue the bookmark onto red wool felt and trim the edges with scallop-edge scissors. For the stitched bookmark, stitch along the center with embroidery floss. Cut a heart from red felt and glue it on the front.

◄ Treat Yourself

Dress up a narrow circular photo frame with candy hearts. Cut out a cardboard circle to fit on the frame. Glue on hearts head-to-head, add a single top layer as shown, then glue the cardboard to the frame.

WELCOME SPRING

The weather gets warmer, the days get brighter, and spirits turn toward sunny spring. As the season of fresh beginnings takes off, steal away with these grand ideas for your home and life.

Green To Envy

A walk through the woods is the perfect time to gather natural souvenirs to turn into easy, high-impact projects that bring the outside in.

Shelf Help

■ Put botanical notecards and prints in mismatched white frames. Hang a couple on the bookcase itself and simply lean the others.

Bottle Brigade

■ Flavored vinegar, olive oil, and clear wine bottles yield shapely, sparkly vases. Choose a variety of sizes, remove the labels, fill them with water, and tuck in fern fronds.

Smart Art

With the spring season comes a slew of timely motifs. Just look out the window and you'll find inspiration for your next do-it-yourself creation.

Botanical Center

■ A dozen garden varieties bloom at this floral workstation. Mount 12-inch-square scrapbook papers onto custom-made wooden boxes, artist's canvases, or foam-core using spray adhesive. Then hang grid-style for big impact.

Butterfly Collection

■ No garden is complete without a butterfly. Mount a collection of colorful butterfly stickers onto a soft-print floral-design paper, and insert into a neutral-tone frame to let the wing colors pop.

Let your home shine with vibrant colors by dying eggs in all your favorite springtime hues.

Eggs of a Different Color

Band Mates

■ To create graphic stripes on dyed eggs, wrap eggs with wide rubber bands (the ones often found on broccoli at the supermarket) before dipping them in dye. If reusing the rubber bands, wash them well between uses to avoid transferring the dye.

Door Prize

■ A tumble of bright eggs makes a cheery welcome. Wrap plastic foam eggs with strips of crepe paper, attaching ends with straight pins. Embellish with ribbons, leaving long tails for hanging. Gather eggs at varying heights and tie ribbons together.

Nesting Instincts

■ Turn a few dyed eggs and bunches of carnations into an eye-catching spring centerpiece. Fill a medium-size footed bowl with a few inches of water. Nestle dyed eggs in a small bowl and set in the center of the footed bowl (prop bowl on a dish if necessary). Cut carnation stems about 2 or 3 inches long and pack the blooms around the bowl of eggs.

Easter Gathering

Easter is a glorious time to celebrate. This light and airy tablescape is laden with fresh-from-the-garden ambience where vegetables, flowers, and bunnies are abundant.

Color Burst

Using a base of white on the table allows the naturally bright spring color palette to pop. For an earthy addition, use jute, natural wicker, and bamboo.

Chair-Back Favors

These petite favors will attract the attention of chocolate lovers on Easter morning. Fill tiny wire baskets with sphagnum moss or Easter grass, then add a handful of foil-wrapped candies. Tie on a big bow made from silk wire-edge ribbon, and attach a basket to each chair back with twine.

Rise and Shine

■ An early-morning breakfast table, outfitted with frolicking porcelain rabbits on a runner of raspberry silk, welcomes family and guests with the colors and icons of spring.

Natural Beauty

■ Elegant china gets a casual treatment when set on woven chargers and topped with a heavy linen napkin tied with twine and one perfect radish. Mixing and matching old glassware in various shapes and sizes is easy when the pieces share a common theme, such as etching or color.

A Shade Greener

■ Artificial lettuce or cabbage leaves carry the nature theme to overhead lighting. Use poster putty to place leaves onto lampshades. For the finishing touch, tie a length of jute around the shade.

Ready to Eat

■ Displayed on a bed of garden lettuce, hard-cooked brown and white eggs are traditional Easter fare. Place the two-tone edible arrangement into a china compote for a classy touch.

Ready to Eat

■ These artificial Brussels sprout-covered topiaries began as 15-inch foam cones potted in a pair of footed soup tureens. Place a piece of foam in the bottom of each tureen to elevate the cone to the lip, then pin or hot-glue the cone onto the foam base. Use long T-shape pins to attach Brussels sprouts to the foam; pin the sprouts as close together as possible, beginning at the bottom and working up. Fill in any open areas with sphagnum moss and tuck, glue, or pin more moss to the bottom edge of each cone. If using fresh sprouts, the topiaries will last unrefrigerated from several days to a week.

Shabby Chic

■ Fresh garden vegetables fill the lower tiers of a wire basket, and flowers nestled in a bed of lettuce top it off with a joyous finale. Wrap the flower stems loosely with a rubber band, and tuck the bouquet into a small canning jar filled with water before hiding it inside the leaves. Soak the vegetables in a chilly bath, then blot them dry and finish the arrangement just before the first guests arrive.

Wrapped Up

■ Here's a change of pace for a plain vase. Dress it up with grosgrain ribbon. Hot-glue one end of the ribbon at the bottom, wrap it around the vase in even overlapping layers, and glue the other end at the top. Add a ribbon tie and pin on a tag. After the flowers fade, the vase makes a cute pencil cup.

Mom

May Day
Surprises

Share the fun of May Day with springy gift packages you can make and give by the dozens.

Two in One

■ Candy, in springtime colors, makes a nice surprise. Place a scoop in a clear cellophane bag tied with ribbon. Nest the bag in a small clay pot and set on a clay drainage plate. Add a couple candies on the plate and get ready to impress.

Mini Masterpieces

■ Before you toss out another pill bottle, look at it with a creative eye. These tiny vessels are just right for delivering a May Day sprig. Cut a strip of scrapbook paper to disguise the bottle and hot-glue it in place overlapping the ends. Tie a ribbon bow around the neck and fill with water and flowers.

Let's Grow

■ Pretty seed packets make a wonderful May Day gift for all your favorite gardeners. Tie three or four packets together with plaid ribbon. Tuck a flower in the back of the ribbon for a fragrant delivery.

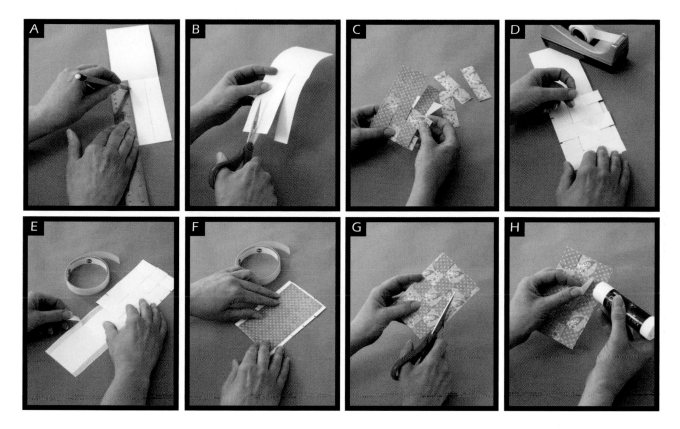

Woven Wonder

■ Transform paper scraps into a treat holder that delivers a message of thoughtfulness.

What You'll Need...

- ☐ 10x3-inch piece of scrapbook paper
- ☐ pencil
- ☐ ruler
- ☐ scissors
- ☐ five 1x3½-inch strips of contrasting scrapbook paper
- ☐ tape
- ☐ double-sided tape
- ☐ glue stick
- ☐ ribbon
- ☐ hot-glue gun and glue sticks

1 Fold the 10x3-inch piece of scrapbook paper in half, short ends together.

2 Unfold strip. On one half, measure and mark three 1-inch-long strips as shown in Photo A.

3 Cut along the marked lines up to the fold as shown in Step B.

4 Weave the five paper strips into the cut piece as shown in Photo C.

5 With the right sides facing down, tape the entire woven section to secure as shown in Photo D.

6 Cut two narrow pieces of double-sided tape the length of the sides as shown in Photo E. Remove backing and press halves together as shown in Photo F.

7 Trim the excess weaving strips from each side as shown in Photo G.

8 Use glue stick to secure loose ends as shown in Photo H.

9 Tie a generous ribbon bow and hot-glue it to the front of the sleeve.

Derby Days

Celebrate the "Run for the Roses" with winning party ideas that are as classy and breathtaking as the event itself. Plastic, glass, and metal horses, found at flea markets and antiques and crafts shops, make for show-stopping decorating.

Trophy Treat Winners

■ Appearing as mini trophies, ordinary boxes wrapped in gold and trimmed with ribbon and braid are a fun way to disguise party mix and candies. Top each stack with a plastic horse that has been spray painted gold. A short length of ribbon hot-glued to the back looks like a saddle blanket.

Out of the Gate

■ Red roses make a fitting centerpiece for a Kentucky Derby party. Make the arrangement unforgettable with a horse figurine bursting from the blooms. To stabilize the horse, wire it to a wooden dowel that is cut to a length approximately three-fourths the height of the bouquet.

Favors Afloat

■ When guests come to the table, give them a small gold-edged pedestal bowl with two white rose buds in which to add their red rose. The napkin tie can be knotted around the base to perfect the favor.

Grand Prize Placesetting

■ The use of metallic gold sets a gilded stage for this rich table. Layer a gold charger with fluted china and top the stack with a horseshoe crafted from embossed wrapping paper (see the pattern on page 156). Nestle a single red rose in a cloth napkin and tie with cording. Allow horses to prance nearby, completing the arrangement with an inviting Mint Julep, the traditional derby drink.

No Photo, No Problem

■ Photo boxes can be used to hold wonderful sentiments. Cut a piece of message scrapbook paper to fit opening. If you can't find message paper, use adhesive letters to portray thoughts. Place the paper under the glass and hot-glue trims on top.

Good Message

Heartfelt Sentiments

■ Dress up heart-shape boxes as gifts or to hold small trinkets inside. With oodles of papers to choose from, you can customize each box.

What You'll Need...

- [ ] heart-shape box
- [ ] pencil
- [ ] scissors
- [ ] scrapbook papers
- [ ] scallop-edge scissors
- [ ] glue stick
- [ ] ice pick
- [ ] scrapbook dimensional brad flowers
- [ ] dimensional lettering
- [ ] hot-glue gun and glue sticks

1 Trace around the lid on the back side of paper; cut out. For the contrasting scalloped edge, trace around the lid on the back side of paper; cut outside the drawn line using scallop-edge scissors. Use a glue stick to adhere the scallop-edge paper to the lid, followed by the top heart. Cut a narrow strip to cover the lid edge; adhere in place.

2 Cut a strip of paper to cover the bottom edge. Adhere paper to box.

3 If lettering is desired; hot-glue letters in place.

4 Use an ice pick to poke holes where flowers are desired. Thread brad prongs through holes and secure prongs on underside of lid.

Boxes

Perfect for celebrating milestones, such as confirmation and first communion, these keepsake boxes are filled with good wishes.

Candy-Filled Maracas

■ Craft colorful party favors that are in keeping with the festive holiday.

What You'll Need...

- [ ] round plastic ornaments with removable toppers
- [ ] plastic paints in blue, green, and white
- [ ] paintbrush
- [ ] scissors
- [ ] braid
- [ ] double-stick tape
- [ ] curling ribbon
- [ ] double-stick tape
- [ ] small candies to fit in ornament
- [ ] wood dowel smaller than ornament opening, cut 6 inches long

1 Remove toppers from ornaments. Wash and dry ornaments thoroughly.

2 Using plastic paint, brush outside of each ornament using X strokes with one color dragged through a little white. Set on end to dry.

3 Cut a piece of braid to wrap around the ornament, allowing ends to overlap slightly. Put double-stick tape on the back of the braid; press onto ornament.

4 Tie curling ribbon around ornament neck; curl with scissors.

5 Fill the ornament with candy.

6 Wrap one end of dowel with double-stick tape until it fits snugly into ornament; press in place.

Fiesta!

Celebrate Cinco de Mayo in style with super salsas and colorful creations inspired by the colors and patterns of Mexico.

Mango Salsa

Orange-Avocado Salsa

    2 medium oranges, peeled, sectioned, and chopped
    1 large ripe avocado, halved, seeded, peeled, and chopped
    ¼ cup chopped red onion
    ¼ cup snipped fresh cilantro
    2 tablespoons lime juice
    ½ to 1 teaspoon bottled hot pepper sauce
    ¼ teaspoon salt

In a medium bowl combine oranges, avocado, onion, cilantro, lime juice, hot pepper sauce, and salt. **Cover and refrigerate** for 2 hours before serving. Makes about 2½ cups.

Mango Salsa

    1 mango, peeled, seeded, and chopped (about 1½ cups)
    1 medium red sweet pepper, seeded and finely chopped
    ¼ cup thinly sliced green onions
    1 Scotch bonnet or hot green chile pepper, seeded and finely chopped*
    3 tablespoons olive oil
    ½ teaspoon finely shredded lime peel
    2 tablespoons lime juice
    1 tablespoon vinegar
    ¼ teaspoon salt
    ¼ teaspoon ground black pepper

In medium bowl combine all ingredients. Store in refrigerator up to 24 hours. Makes 2 cups.
*NOTE: See tip for handling chile peppers, page 55.

Orange-Avocado Salsa

You're Invited

Welcome guests to a Cinco de Mayo party with brightly adorned invitations. Use double-sided tape to attach ribbon and rickrack to the front of a plain card stock note as shown. Fringe the bottom edge with scissors. Choose bright adhesive letters to spell out "fiesta" across the front and write party details on the inside.

Watermelon Salsa

- 2 cups chopped seeded watermelon
- ½ cup chopped cucumber
- ½ cup chopped orange or yellow sweet pepper
- ½ of an ear fresh sweet corn, cut from the cob
- 2 tablespoons chopped fresh cilantro
- 1 to 2 jalapeño chile peppers, seeded and chopped*
- 1 tablespoon finely chopped red onion
- 1 teaspoon finely shredded lime peel
- ¼ cup lime juice
- 1 teaspoon packed brown sugar
- ¼ teaspoon salt
- ¼ teaspoon crushed red pepper

In a medium bowl combine watermelon, cucumber, sweet pepper, corn, cilantro, jalapeño pepper(s), and onion.
In a small bowl combine lime peel, lime juice, brown sugar, salt, and crushed red pepper. Add lime mixture to watermelon mixture and toss to coat.
Cover and chill in the refrigerator for 1 hour to let flavors combine. Makes 3½ cups.

Black Bean Salsa

- 1 15-ounce can black beans, rinsed and drained
- 1 medium cucumber, peeled, seeded and chopped
- 1 medium tomato, seeded and chopped
- ½ cup sliced green onions
- ¼ cup lime juice
- 1 tablespoon snipped fresh cilantro
- 1 tablespoon olive oil
- ½ teaspoon ground cumin
- ⅛ teaspoon salt
- ⅛ teaspoon cayenne pepper

In a medium bowl combine black beans, cucumber, tomato, green onions, lime juice, cilantro, oil, cumin, salt, and cayenne pepper.
Cover and chill in the refrigerator for 4 to 24 hours. Serve with a slotted spoon over grilled pork, smoked bratwursts or sausages, grilled chicken or salmon. Makes about 3½ cups.

Fresh Cherry Salsa

- 2 tablespoons boiling water
- 1 teaspoon crushed red pepper
- 2 cups halved and pitted red sweet cherries
- ⅓ cup finely chopped red sweet pepper
- ⅓ cup finely chopped red onion
- 2 tablespoons lime juice
- 1 tablespoon sugar
- 1 teaspoon kosher salt
- 1 tablespoon snipped fresh cilantro

In a medium bowl combine the water and crushed pepper. Set aside for 5 minutes for crushed pepper to soften. Stir in cherries, sweet pepper, onion, lime juice, sugar, and salt.
Toss mixture together. Allow mixture to stand for 30 minutes before serving. Stir in cilantro just before serving. Makes about 3 cups.

> ***TEST KITCHEN TIP:** Because chile peppers contain volatile oils that can burn your skin and eyes, avoid direct contact with them as much as possible. When working with chile peppers, wear plastic or rubber gloves. If your bare hands do touch the peppers, wash your hands and nails well with soap and water.

Service
With a Smile

Surprise Mom this Mother's Day with a gorgeous one-of-a-kind ceramic platter that she can use and display all year.

Mini Masterpieces

■ While this design may look complicated, it's simply a series of circles, dots, lines, and petal shapes. Once the large circles are painted, outline them with petal strokes. Paint stems and oval leaves. Fill in the background with smaller flowers as shown; let dry. To add detail, add small black dots by dipping a pencil eraser or paintbrush handle end into paint then dotting on the platter. Use a flat brush to create a checked border around the dish edge. Whether you paint this platter at home using glass paints or work it up at a paint-your-own-pottery shop, Mom will see your love shine through every paint stroke.

Hats Off
to Spring

Hats of every kind set the stage for a springtime get together. Whether it's hats off to the grad, an upcoming bride, or just to welcome in the season, have fun decorating with this unexpectedly fun theme.

The Write Stuff

■ Used as grad party invitations or as thank-yous, these his and hers cards set the tone of the party. Start with plain card stock notes, then use the patterns on page 156 to cut the hats from scrapbook paper. Glue stick adheres the hats to the note cards while hot glue secures button, ribbon, and feather trims.

Bonnet Bouquet

■ Springtime hats and fresh-cut flowers combine to make a stunning centerpiece. Use floral water tubes to keep the blooms perky and crystal vases to prop the hats at varying levels.

Open House

Turn to the school's color palette to make easy-do accents for a graduation gathering. These simple touches brighten the day in a special way.

School Flags

■ When you serve food graduation-style, offer bite-size portions. Hold tidbits together using mini flags in school colors. Cut short ribbon lengths with pinking shears and glue around wooden picks to make flags for sliders, sandwiches, and rollups.

Mortar Board Buttercakes

    1 cup (2 sticks) butter, softened
1⅓ cups sugar
    3 eggs
    2 teaspoons vanilla
    2 cups all-purpose flour
    2 teaspoons baking powder
 ½ teaspoon baking soda
 ¼ teaspoon salt
 ⅔ cup buttermilk
    Sour Cream Frosting

Preheat oven to 350°F. Line twenty-four 2½-inch muffin cups with paper bake cups.

In a large mixing bowl beat butter with electric mixer on medium-high for about 1 minute. Add sugar. Beat until light and fluffy. Add eggs, one at a time, beating well after each addition. Beat in vanilla. Whisk together flour, baking powder, soda, and salt. Add flour mixture in two additions, alternating with buttermilk, and beating on low after each addition until combined.

Fill lined cups about two-thirds full. Bake for 15 to 18 minutes or until a toothpick inserted in center comes out clean. Cool in pans on a wire rack for 5 minutes. Remove cupcakes from pan; cool completely on wire rack. Makes 24 cupcakes.

Mortar Board Buttercakes

SOUR CREAM FROSTING: In a large mixing bowl beat ½ cup (1 stick) softened butter with mixer 30 seconds; beat in one 8-ounce carton sour cream. Gradually beat in one 2-pound bag powdered sugar. Beat in 1 teaspoon vanilla and 1 tablespoon milk. Use immediately or cover and refrigerate for up to 3 days. Remove frosting from refrigerator and let stand at room temperature for 30 minutes before using. Frost cupcakes with a knife, or spoon frosting into a large resealable plastic bag. Snip one corner of bag and squeeze to pipe onto cupcakes.

Pour nonpareils into a shallow dish. Roll edge of cupcakes in nonpareils to make colored rim, using your hands to help nonpareils stick to frosting if needed. For toppers, place 4 ounces semisweet chocolate in small microwave-safe bowl. Microwave on 100% power (high) for 2 minutes, stirring every 30 seconds until melted. Dip small crackers, such as Wheat Thins in melted chocolate. Immediately place on chocolate-covered cherry, and top with a mini M&M and fruit leather cut to resemble a tassel. Place cupcakes in covered container and refrigerate until set or up to 3 days.

Beginning Gardener ▶
Share the love of gardening with children. Get them started with seed packets taped to skewers, kid-size tools, and a pair of boots for tromping in the dirt.

Easy Does It
Suprises to Boot

◀ Easter Boot
Skip the basket this year and let the Easter Bunny plant his goodies in springtime boots that are a gift in themselves. Fill the bottoms with tissue paper, adding shredded grass at the top before filling with holiday surprises.

Goodies to Go

For unexpected gift wrap, plant skewered candies and cookies in a boot stuffed with a plastic foam ball. Hide the foam ball with scrunched cellophane and add a ribbon bow to complete the gift.

This cute display will get rave reviews all season long. Place a vase, glass, or jar inside the boot and fill with water. Place a fresh-flower arrangement inside, allowing leaves to trail down the sides. Make one for yourself and give the other one away.

◄ **Artful Arrangement**

Here's a fun way to keep art supplies organized and at hand. Pour sand in the bottom of each boot to act as a weight and to help supplies stand upright.

Thai Chicken Burgers
recipe, page 75

SAVOR THE SEASON

Let these fabulous recipes be the highlight of your seasonal celebrations, including bridal or baby showers, backyard grill outs, and neighborhood block parties.

The Berry Best

This time of year is bursting with berries and celebrations. From wedding showers to Mother's Day, luscious desserts make the occasions truly splendid.

Vanilla Cake with Buttercream, Berries, and Jam

Vanilla Cake with Buttercream, Berries, and Jam

2½ cups all-purpose flour
⅓ cup cornstarch
3½ teaspoons baking powder
1 teaspoon salt
¾ cup water
⅔ cup vegetable oil
½ cup milk
1 tablespoon vanilla
4 egg whites
¼ teaspoon cream of tartar
1½ cups sugar
   Butter Frosting
1 cup strawberry jam
3 cups sliced fresh strawberries or whole raspberries, blackberries, and/or blueberries
1 cup whole fresh strawberries, raspberries, blackberries, and/or blueberries

Preheat oven to 350°F. Grease bottoms of two 8×1½-inch round cake pans. Line bottoms of pans with waxed paper; grease and flour pans. Set pans aside.

In a large bowl stir together flour, cornstarch, baking powder, and salt. Add the water, oil, milk, and vanilla. Beat with a wire whisk until smooth.

In a medium mixing bowl combine egg whites and cream of tartar. Beat with an electric mixer on medium speed until soft peaks form (tips curl). Gradually add sugar, beating on high speed until stiff peaks form (tips stand straight). Fold beaten egg whites into batter. Spread batter evenly into prepared pans.

Bake for 22 to 25 minutes or until a wooden toothpick inserted near centers comes out clean. Cool in pans on wire racks for 10 minutes. Remove cakes from pans and cool completely on wire racks.

To assemble, cut cake layers in half horizontally. Place one cake layer, cut side down, on a serving plate. Spread with ¾ cup of the Butter Frosting then ¼ cup of the jam. Top with 1 cup of the sliced berries. Repeat with two more cake layers, frosting, jam, and sliced berries. Top with the final cake layer, cut side down. Spread with remaining frosting and jam. Top with whole berries. Makes 12 servings.

BUTTER FROSTING: In a medium mixing bowl beat ½ cup softened butter with an electric mixer on medium speed for 30 seconds. Gradually add 3 cups powdered sugar, beating well. Slowly beat in 3 tablespoons milk and 2 teaspoons vanilla. Gradually beat in 3 cups additional powdered sugar. If necessary, beat in additional milk, 1 teaspoon at a time, to reach spreading consistency.

Berry-Cornmeal Shortcakes

Berry-Cornmeal Shortcakes

1 pound small fresh strawberries, blueberries, raspberries, and/or blackberries (halve large berries)
¼ cup orange marmalade
2 tablespoons finely snipped crystallized ginger
1¾ cups all-purpose flour
½ cup cornmeal
2 teaspoons baking powder
½ teaspoon salt
10 tablespoons butter
¾ to 1 cup whipping cream
2 tablespoons butter, melted
1 cup whipping cream
2 tablespoons sugar
1 teaspoon finely shredded orange peel

Combine berries, marmalade, and crystallized ginger. Cover and let stand at room temperature for 30 to 60 minutes.

White Cheesecake with
Raspberry Sauce

Preheat oven to 425°F. Line a baking sheet with parchment paper or foil (or lightly grease a baking sheet); set aside.

In a large bowl stir together flour, cornmeal, baking powder, and salt. Using a pastry blender, cut in the 10 tablespoons butter until mixture resembles coarse crumbs. Add the ¾ cup of the cream, stirring with a fork just until moistened. (If necessary, stir in additional cream, 1 tablespoon at a time, to moisten.)

Turn dough out onto a lightly floured surface. Gently knead for four to six strokes or just until a ball forms. Pat or lightly roll dough to about ½ inch thickness. Using a floured 3-inch round biscuit cutter, cut dough into 8 circles, dipping cutter into flour between cuts to prevent sticking. Place dough circles on prepared baking sheet. Brush tops with the 2 tablespoons melted butter. Bake for 15 to 18 minutes or until golden. Brush with any remaining melted butter. Cool shortcakes on a wire rack.

In a medium mixing bowl combine the 1 cup cream, sugar, and orange peel. Beat with electric mixer on medium to high speed just until stiff peaks form (tips stand straight).

To serve, split shortcakes in two. Spoon berry mixture on bottoms of shortcakes. Top with whipped cream and replace tops of shortcakes. Makes 8 servings.

White Cheesecake with Raspberry Sauce.

1 cup crushed shortbread cookies
3 tablespoons finely chopped toasted slivered almonds
¼ cup butter, melted
2 8-ounce packages cream cheese, softened

Lemon-Blackberry Mini Tarts

6 ounces white baking chocolate with cocoa butter, melted and cooled
½ cup sugar
⅔ cup sour cream
1 teaspoon vanilla
3 eggs
½ cup fresh or frozen raspberries, thawed
Raspberry Sauce
White baking chocolate with cocoa butter, grated (optional)

Preheat oven to 350°F. For crust, in a small bowl combine crushed cookies and almonds. Drizzle with melted butter; toss gently to coat. Press mixture evenly onto bottom of an 8-inch springform pan; set aside.

For filling, in a large mixing bowl combine cream cheese and melted white chocolate. Beat with an electric mixer on medium-high speed until combined. Add sugar, sour cream, and vanilla; beat until fluffy. Add eggs; beat on low just until combined. Pour filling over crust, spreading evenly. Place springform pan in a shallow baking pan.

Bake about 45 minutes or until a 2½-inch area around the edge appears set and the center appears nearly set when gently shaken.

Cool in pan on a wire rack for 15 minutes. Loosen edge of cheesecake from side of pan and cool for 30 minutes. Remove side of pan; cool completely on rack (about

1¼ hours). Cover and chill for 4 to 24 hours.

To serve, top cheesecake with raspberries and drizzle with Raspberry Sauce. If desired, sprinkle with grated white chocolate. Makes 12 servings.

RASPBERRY SAUCE: In a small saucepan heat one 10-ounce jar seedless red raspberry preserves over low heat until melted. Bring just to simmering, stirring gently; cool. If desired, stir in 1 to 2 tablespoons raspberry liqueur. Cover and chill until ready to serve. Makes 1 cup.

Lemon-Blackberry Mini Tarts

½ of a 15-ounce package rolled refrigerated unbaked piecrust (1 crust)
½ of an 8-ounce package cream cheese, softened
¼ cup lemon curd
1 cup fresh blackberries
2 tablespoons seedless blackberry spreadable fruit
2 teaspoons lemon juice
Powdered sugar
Fresh mint sprigs

Preheat oven to 400°F. Let piecrust stand according to package directions. On a lightly floured surface, unroll piecrust. Cut into four 4½- to 5-inch circles. Transfer pastry circles to four 3½- to 4-inch tart pans that have removable bottoms. Press pastry into fluted sides of pans; trim pastry even with rims. Prick bottoms of tart shells with a fork. Place tart pans on a baking sheet. Bake for 10 to 12 minutes or until pastry is golden. Cool on a wire rack.

For filling, in a small mixing bowl combine cream cheese and lemon curd. Beat with an electric mixer on medium speed until smooth. Spread

Strawberry Meringue Pie

70 CELEBRATE

filling evenly in baked tart shells. Cover and chill for 2 to 24 hours.

To serve, remove tarts from pans. Arrange blackberries on tarts. In a small bowl combine spreadable fruit and lemon juice; spoon over tarts. Sprinkle with powdered sugar and garnish with mint. Makes 4 servings.

Strawberry Meringue Pie

1 rolled refrigerated unbaked piecrust (½ of a 15-ounce package)
3 egg whites
½ teaspoon vanilla
¼ teaspoon cream of tartar
½ cup sugar
7 tablespoons lemon curd
5 cups fresh strawberries (halve large berries)
Snipped fresh mint

Let unbaked crust stand at room temperature according to package directions. Place egg whites in a large mixing bowl; let stand at room temperature for 30 minutes.

Preheat oven to 450°F. Unroll and line a 9-inch pie plate with crust; flute edge, if desired. Prick bottom and sides with a fork. Bake for 10 to 12 minutes or until golden. Remove from oven; cool on a wire rack. Reduce oven temperature to 300°F.

For meringue layer, add vanilla and cream of tartar to egg whites. Beat with an electric mixer on medium until soft peaks form. Gradually add sugar. Beat on high until stiff peaks form and sugar is almost dissolved. Spread in baked piecrust, building up meringue along edges. Bake for 35 minutes. Cool on a wire rack. Meringue will fall slightly.

In a large microwave-safe bowl heat lemon curd in microwave on 50% power (medium) for 15 to

Strawberry Fritters

20 seconds. Spread 4 tablespoons warm curd on meringue. Add berries to remaining lemon curd; lightly stir to coat. Spoon into pie shell. Refrigerate for 30 to 60 minutes. To serve, top with fresh mint. Cut with serrated knife. Makes 8 servings.

Strawberry Fritters

16 medium strawberries (about 1 pint)
16 4-inch bamboo or wooden skewers
¼ cup honey mustard
¼ cup slivered almonds, toasted and chopped
¼ cup crushed saltine crackers (about 7 crackers)
Cooking oil for deep-fat frying

Wash strawberries and thoroughly dry. Insert a skewer through the top of each berry; set aside.

Place honey mustard in a small bowl. Combine almonds and crackers in another small bowl. Dip or spread bottom two-thirds of each berry with honey mustard; roll in almond mixture, coating well.

In a deep-fat fryer heat 2 inches cooking oil to 365°F. Fry strawberries, two at a time, for 15 seconds. Carefully remove berries with tongs, gripping the end of the skewer or the uncoated portion of the berry. Drain on paper towels. Serve berries within 30 minutes of frying. Makes 16 appetizer servings.

Grill & Chill

Invite friends over to savor succulent grilled meat, garden-fresh sides, and a summer-perfect dessert.

Thai Chicken Burgers
recipe, page 75

Summer Peach Pie Twisters recipe, page 75

Honey-Glazed Chicken
with Roasted Grapes

Thai Chicken Burgers

Pictured on page 72.

- ¾ cup panko (Japanese-style bread crumbs)
- 2 tablespoons peanut butter
- 2 tablespoons lime juice
- 2 tablespoons toasted sesame oil
- 1 tablespoon finely chopped green onion
- 1 tablespoon soy sauce
- 1 tablespoon red curry paste
- 2 teaspoons grated fresh ginger
- 3 cloves garlic, minced
- 1 pound uncooked ground chicken
- 1 small cucumber, halved lengthwise, seeded, and thinly sliced
- ½ cup mayonnaise
- ¼ cup coconut, toasted
- ¼ cup loosely packed fresh mint leaves, snipped
- 4 seeded hamburger buns, split and toasted
  Fresh cilantro leaves (optional)

In a large bowl combine bread crumbs, peanut butter, lime juice, 1 tablespoon of the sesame oil, the green onion, soy sauce, curry paste, ginger, and garlic. Add ground chicken; mix well. Shape mixture into four ¾-inch-thick patties. Cover and chill until needed.

In a small bowl combine cucumber, mayonnaise, coconut, and mint. Cover and chill until ready to serve. Brush patties lightly with the remaining 1 tablespoon sesame oil.

For a charcoal grill, grill patties on the rack of an uncovered grill directly over medium coals for 14 to 18 minutes or until no longer pink (165°F), turning once halfway through grilling. (For a gas grill, preheat grill. Reduce heat to medium. Place patties on grill rack over heat. Cover and grill as above.)

Serve burgers in buns with cucumber mixture. If desired, serve with cilantro. Makes 4 servings.

Summer Peach Pie Twisters

Pictured on page 73.

- 1 15-ounce package rolled refrigerated unbaked piecrust (2 crusts)
- 3 medium peaches, pitted and chopped, or one 16-ounce package frozen unsweetened peach slices, thawed and chopped
- ⅔ cup tiny marshmallows
- ½ teaspoon cinnamon sugar
- 1 tablespoon cinnamon sugar
  Vanilla ice Cream (optional)

Let piecrusts stand at room temperature according to package directions. Preheat oven to 400°F. Line two large baking sheets with parchment paper or foil; lightly grease the foil if using. Set aside.

In medium bowl combine peaches, marshmallows, and the ½ teaspoon cinnamon sugar.

Unroll 1 piecrust. Cut crust in 6 wedges. Spoon a scant ¼ cup of the peach mixture along one long side of each wedge, ½ inch from edge of crust. Brush edge of long sides of crust with a little water. Fold crust over filling. Using the tines of a fork, press long sides together to seal. Fold the top edge of the crust back to expose some of the filling.

Place pies on prepared baking sheets. Prick top crusts of pies two or three times with a fork. Sprinkle with the 1 tablespoon cinnamon sugar. Bake for 15 to 18 minutes or until filling is bubbly and pastry is golden brown. Slightly cool the pies on pans to serve warm, or cool the pies completely.

Serve pies standing upright in paper cups or in glasses. Serve with a scoop of ice cream, if desired. Makes 12 twisters.

Honey-Glazed Chicken with Roasted Grapes

- 4 bone-in chicken breast halves (2½ to 3 pounds total)
- 5 tablespoons balsamic vinegar
- 1 tablespoon extra-virgin olive oil
- 3 garlic cloves, minced
- ¾ teaspoon salt
- ¼ teaspoon ground black pepper
- ¼ cup honey
- 2 teaspoons freshly shredded orange peel
- 1 bulb garlic (about 10 cloves)
- 2 teaspoons extra-virgin olive oil
- 1 pound red and/or green seedless grapes, cut into 4 bunches
- 1 tablespoon honey
- 1 wedge blue cheese (optional)
- 1 tablespoon honey (optional)

Place chicken in a large resealable plastic bag set in a shallow dish. For marinade, combine 2 tablespoons of the vinegar, 1 tablespoon oil, minced garlic, ½ teaspoon of the salt, and the pepper. Pour marinade over chicken. Seal bag and turn bag to coat chicken. Set aside for 15 minutes.

Meanwhile, stir together the remaining 3 tablespoons vinegar, ¼ cup honey, the orange peel, and the remaining ¼ teaspoon salt; set aside. Separate and peel garlic cloves; place on an 8-inch square of heavy foil; drizzle with 2 teaspoons olive oil. Wrap foil around garlic to seal.

For a charcoal grill, arrange preheated coals around a drip pan. Test for medium heat above the pan. Remove chicken from bag or bowl, discarding marinade. Place chicken, skin sides down, on the grill rack over the drip pan. Place garlic packet next to chicken. Grill, covered, for 25 minutes. Remove garlic and cool. Turn chicken skin sides up; brush with some of the honey mixture. Cover and grill about 25 minutes more or until chicken is no longer pink (170°F), brushing occasionally with

Corn Salad

honey mixture up until last 5 minutes of grilling. (For a gas grill, preheat grill. Reduce heat to medium and adjust for indirect cooking. Place chicken, skin sides down, on grill rack. Cover; grill as above.)

Meanwhile, drizzle grapes with 1 tablespoon honey. Place grapes on grill rack over coals or heat. Cover and grill for 2 to 3 minutes or until browned and softened, turning once.

Transfer chicken and grapes to a serving platter. If desired, serve with cheese topped with garlic and drizzled with honey. Makes 4 servings.

Tuscan Spit-Roasted Pork Loin

  1 3- to 4-pound boneless pork top
     loin roast (single loin)
  8 cloves garlic, minced
  2 tablespoons snipped fresh
     rosemary
  4 teaspoons finely shredded
     lemon peel
  2 teaspoons kosher salt
  1 teaspoon ground black pepper

  3 tablespoons olive oil
     Grilled lemon halves (optional)
     Fresh Italian parsley sprigs
     (optional)

Trim fat from meat. Using the tip of a sharp knife, cut 1½-inch-deep slits into the pork at 2- to 3-inch intervals.

Using a mortar and pestle, mash together garlic, rosemary, lemon peel, salt, and pepper until a paste forms. Slowly add olive oil to the mixture, mashing until combined.

Using your fingers, press garlic paste into the slits in the pork, making sure to press paste all the way into slits. Rub any remaining paste on the roast.

To secure the roast on a spit rod, place one holding fork on the rod, tines toward the point. Insert rod through the narrow end of the roast, pressing the tines of the holding fork firmly into meat. Place second holding fork on rod with tines toward roast; press tines of holding fork firmly into meat. Adjust forks and tighten screws. Test balance, making adjustments as necessary.

For a charcoal grill, arrange medium coals around a drip pan. Test for medium-low heat above the pan. Attach spit; turn on the motor and lower the grill hood. Let the roast rotate over the drip pan for 1½ to 2 hours or until an instant-read thermometer inserted into the center of the roast registers 155°F. Add hot coals as needed to maintain temperature. (For a gas grill, preheat grill. Reduce heat to medium-low. Adjust for indirect cooking. Grill as above.)

Remove roast from spit. Cover with foil. Let stand for 15 minutes. The temperature of the meat after standing should be 160°F.

If desired, serve roast with grilled lemon halves and parsley sprigs. Makes 8 to 10 servings.

Corn Salad

  4   tablespoons lime juice
  1   tablespoon honey
  1   jalapeño pepper, seeded and
      finely chopped*
  3   tablespoons snipped fresh
      cilantro or 1 tablespoon snipped
      fresh mint
  ¼   teaspoon salt
  6   fresh ears of corn
  1½ cups fresh baby spinach
  1   large tomato, seeded and
      chopped
  ¾   cup seeded, chopped cucumber
      Small fresh peppers, optional

In a large bowl whisk together lime juice and honey until combined. Stir in jalapeño pepper, cilantro, and salt. Cut corn kernels off cobs; add to lime juice mixture. Stir in spinach, tomato, and cucumber. Garnish with whole peppers, if desired. Serve immediately or cover and chill for up to 1 hour. Makes 9 servings.

*NOTE: See tip for handling chile peppers, page 55.

Smoked Paprika Flank Steak with Basil Butter

Smoked Paprika Flank Steak with Basil Butter

1½ pounds beef flank steak
¼ cup balsamic vinegar or sherry vinegar
2 tablespoons vegetable oil
2 teaspoons smoked paprika
½ teaspoon kosher salt or salt
Basil Butter

Trim fat from meat. Score both sides of meat in a diamond pattern by making shallow diagonal cuts at 1-inch intervals. Place meat in a resealable plastic bag set in a shallow dish.

For marinade, in a small bowl combine vinegar, oil, smoked paprika, and salt. Pour marinade over meat. Seal bag; turn to coat meat. Marinate in the refrigerator for 4 to 24 hours, turning bag occasionally to distribute marinade. Drain meat, reserving marinade.

For a charcoal grill, grill meat on the rack of an uncovered grill directly over medium coals for 17 to 21 minutes for medium (160° F), turning and brushing once with the reserved marinade halfway through grilling. (For a gas grill, preheat grill. Reduce heat to medium. Place meat on grill rack over heat. Cover and grill as above.) Discard any remaining marinade.

Thinly slice meat diagonally across the grain. Immediately top meat slices with Basil Butter. Makes 6 servings.

BASIL BUTTER: In a small bowl combine ¼ cup softened butter; 2 tablespoons snipped fresh basil; 1 clove garlic, minced; ½ teaspoon Dijon-style mustard; ¼ teaspoon smoked paprika; and ¼ teaspoon ground black pepper. Shape into a 1½-inch-diameter log. Wrap in plastic wrap and chill for at least 2 hours. Let stand at room temperature for 20 minutes before serving. Cut into slices.

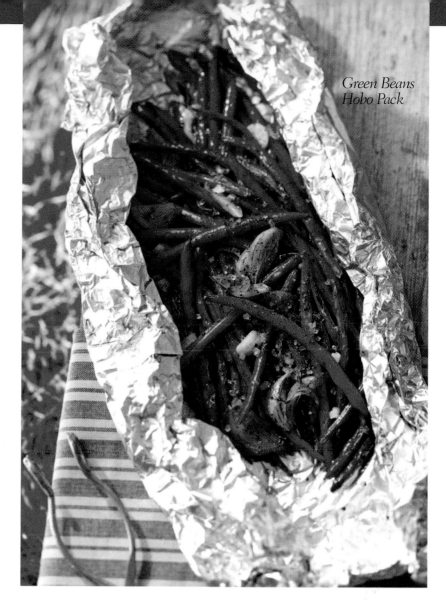

Green Beans Hobo Pack

Green Beans Hobo Pack

1 pound green beans and/or wax beans
1 small shallot, thinly sliced
2 cloves garlic, thinly sliced
¼ teaspoon salt
¼ teaspoon ground black pepper
1 tablespoon olive oil
Coarse salt (optional)
Coarse ground black pepper (optional)

Fold a 36×18-inch piece of heavy foil in half to an 18-inch square. If desired, trim beans.

Place beans, shallot, and garlic in the center of foil. Sprinkle with ¼ teaspoon salt and ¼ teaspoon pepper; drizzle with oil. Bring up two opposite edges of foil; seal with a double fold. Fold the remaining ends to completely enclose vegetables, leaving space for steam to build.

For a charcoal grill, grill vegetable packet on the rack of an uncovered grill directly over medium coals for 25 to 30 minutes or until vegetables are tender, turning occasionally. (For a gas grill, preheat grill. Reduce heat to medium. Place vegetable packet on grill rack over heat. Cover and grill as above.) If desired, sprinkle with salt and pepper. Makes 4 servings.

Two-Tone Coleslaw

Pride of the Potluck

Share one of these crowd-pleasers at your next gathering.

Two-Tone Coleslaw

⅔ cup light mayonnaise
3 tablespoons cider vinegar
1 tablespoon snipped fresh dill or
   1 teaspoon dried dillweed
½ teaspoon salt
½ teaspoon coarsely ground black
   pepper
7 cups shredded green cabbage
3 medium apples, cored and thinly
   sliced
1 cup chopped sweet onion
   Fresh dill sprig, optional

For dressing, in an extra-large bowl stir together mayonnaise, vinegar, dill, salt, and pepper. Stir in cabbage, apples, and onion. Cover and chill at least 2 hours or up to 48 hours. If desired, garnish with fresh dill. Makes 12 servings.

Greek Pasta Salad

Greek Pasta Salad

12 ounces dried mostaccioli or
   penne (about 4 cups uncooked)
2 cups cherry tomatoes, quartered
1 medium cucumber, halved
   lengthwise and sliced
4 green onions, sliced
⅓ cup pitted Kalamata olives,
   halved
½ cup olive oil
½ cup lemon juice
2 tablespoons snipped fresh basil
   or 2 teaspoons dried basil,
   crushed
2 tablespoons snipped fresh
   oregano or 2 teaspoons dried
   oregano, crushed
1 tablespoon anchovy paste
   (optional)
4 to 6 cloves garlic, minced
¼ teaspoon salt
¼ teaspoon ground black pepper
1 cup crumbled feta cheese
   (4 ounces)
   Fresh oregano leaves

Cook pasta according to package directions. Drain in a colander. Rinse pasta with cold water; drain again.

In a large bowl toss together the cooked pasta, tomatoes, cucumber, green onions, and olives.
In a screw-top jar combine the olive oil, lemon juice, basil, the 2 tablespoons oregano, anchovy paste (if using), garlic, salt, and pepper. Cover; shake well. Drizzle over pasta mixture; toss to coat.
Cover and chill for at least 2 hours or up to 24 hours. To serve, add feta cheese; toss. Sprinkle with oregano leaves. Makes 12 to 16 servings.

Cream Cheese and Vegetable Pizza Appetizer

Cream Cheese and Vegetable Pizza Appetizer

When you're in a hurry, stop by your supermarket salad bar to pick up cut vegetables.

- 2 8-ounce packages refrigerated crescent rolls (8 rolls each)
- 2 8-ounce packages cream cheese, softened
- 1 cup mayonnaise or salad dressing*
- 1 0.4-ounce package dry buttermilk ranch salad dressing mix
- 4 cups cut-up raw vegetables (such as broccoli, cauliflower, carrots, and celery)
- 1½ cups shredded cheddar cheese (6 ounces)

Preheat oven to 375°F. For crust, separate crescent rolls into four 4-roll rectangles and press into the bottom and up the sides of an ungreased 15×10×1-inch baking pan, pressing perforations to seal. Bake for 10 to 12 minutes or until golden. Cool the crust in the pan on a wire rack.

In a mixing bowl beat together the cream cheese, mayonnaise, and dry dressing mix until well combined.

Spread the cream cheese mixture on the cooled crust. Top with assorted vegetables and sprinkle with cheese. Press lightly.

Cover and chill for at least 1 hour or up to 24 hours. Cut pizza into squares to serve. Store any leftover appetizers in the refrigerator. Makes 35 appetizer servings.

***NOTE:** If you like, decrease the mayonnaise to ½ cup and add ½ cup sour cream.

Layered California-Style BLT Salad

Bring out the beauty of this West Coast concoction by treating it to a tumble of buttery rich avocado slices. Slice the avocados just before serving.

- 2 12-ounce packages applewood-smoked bacon
  Garlicky Focaccia Croutons
- 4 cups shredded romaine lettuce
- 4 cups baby spinach leaves
- 6 medium red and/or yellow heirloom tomatoes, cored, quartered, and sliced ½ inch thick (3 cups)
  Dilled Avocado Dressing

Cook bacon in batches over medium heat until crisp. Drain bacon on paper towels. When cool, coarsely crumble bacon. Set aside.

In a 3- to 4-quart glass bowl arrange half the Garlicky Focaccia Croutons. Top with half the romaine and half the spinach. Top with half the tomato slices and half the bacon. Spread half the Dilled Avocado Dressing over bacon, sealing dressing to edge of bowl. Repeat layers, ending with dressing. Cover and chill for up to 8 hours. Makes 12 servings.

GARLICKY FOCACCIA CROUTONS: Preheat oven to 300°F. Combine 3 cups of ½-inch cubes garlic foccacia and 2 tablespoons olive oil; toss to coat. Spread bread cubes evenly in a 15×10×1-inch baking pan. Bake for about 20 minutes or until cubes are crisp, stirring once; cool.

DILLED AVOCADO DRESSING: In a blender or food processor combine 1 ripe avocado, halved, seeded, peeled, and mashed; ½ cup mayonnaise; ½ cup sour cream; 3 tablespoons freshly squeezed lemon juice; 3 tablespoons snipped fresh dill; ¼ cup milk; ½ teaspoon garlic salt; and ¼ teaspoon ground black pepper. Cover and blend until smooth.

Layered California-Style BLT Salad

Ranch Deviled Egg Bites

and egg white halves. Cover and chill for up to 8 hours. If desired, serve with sliced olives and garnish with cilantro leaves. Makes 14 servings.
*NOTE: Because chile peppers contain volatile oils that can burn your skin and eyes, avoid direct contact with them as much as possible. When working with chile peppers, wear plastic or rubber gloves. If your bare hands do touch the peppers, wash your hands and nails well with soap and warm water.

Classic Potato Salad

  2 pounds potatoes (6 medium)
  ¼ teaspoon salt
1¼ cups mayonnaise or salad
       dressing
  1 tablespoon yellow mustard
  ½ teaspoon salt
  ¼ teaspoon black pepper
  1 cup thinly sliced celery (2 stalks)
  ⅓ cup chopped onion (1 small)
  ½ cup chopped sweet or dill pickles
       or sweet or dill pickle relish
  6 hard-cooked eggs, coarsely
       chopped

In a large saucepan place potatoes, the ¼ teaspoon salt, and enough water to cover. Bring to boiling; reduce heat. Simmer, covered, for 20 to 25 minutes or just until tender. Drain well; cool slightly. Peel and cube the potatoes.

For dressing, in a large bowl combine mayonnaise, mustard, the ½ teaspoon salt, and the pepper. Stir in celery, onion, and pickles. Add potatoes and eggs. Toss lightly to coat. Cover and chill for 6 to 24 hours.

To serve, transfer the potato salad to a salad bowl. If desired, sprinkle with additional black pepper. Makes about 14 servings.

Ranch Deviled Egg Bites

       Nonstick cooking spray
  4 jalapeño chile peppers*
  4 roma tomatoes, halved
  8 hard-cooked eggs, peeled
       and halved
  ½ cup plain Greek yogurt
  2 tablespoons snipped fresh
       cilantro
  ¼ cup thinly sliced green onions (2)
  1 1-ounce package ranch dry
       salad dressing mix
  3 tablespoons olive oil
       Garlic-stuffed green olives, sliced
       (optional)
       Fresh cilantro leaves (optional)

Coat a small skillet with cooking spray; heat skillet over medium heat. Add peppers to skillet; cook about 5 minutes or until lightly charred, turning occasionally. Let peppers stand until cool enough to handle. Halve peppers lengthwise; remove seeds and membranes. Scoop out and discard pulp from tomato halves. Set pepper and tomato halves aside.

Remove yolks from eggs and place in a medium bowl. Add 4 of the egg white halves to bowl; mash with a fork. Stir in yogurt, cilantro, green onions, dressing mix, and oil. Spoon yolk mixture into jalapeño, tomato,

Classic Potato Salad

Chocolate Temptations

Decadent candies, cookies, bars, and brownies will have friends and family raving.

Oat 'n' Toffee Grahams

Oat 'n' Toffee Grahams

This chocolate-layered graham cracker treat is super easy to make and sturdy enough for packaging—if you're looking for bake sale or food gift ideas.

- 12 whole graham crackers (rectangles)
- 1½ cups rolled oats
- ¾ cup granulated sugar
- ¾ cup packed brown sugar
- 3 tablespoons all-purpose flour
- ⅔ cup butter, melted
- 1 egg, lightly beaten
- 1 teaspoon vanilla
- 1 12-ounce package (2 cups) semisweet chocolate pieces
- ½ cup smokehouse-flavor whole almonds, coarsely chopped

Preheat oven to 350°F. Line a 15×10×1-inch baking pan with foil, extending foil over the edges of the pan. Arrange graham crackers in a single layer in prepared pan.

In a large bowl stir together the oats, granulated sugar, brown sugar, and flour. Add butter, egg, and vanilla; stir until well combined.

Spoon oats mixture over graham crackers, spreading mixture evenly to edges of pan.

Bake for 20 to 25 minutes or until oat mixture bubbles and is light brown on top. Remove from oven; sprinkle with chocolate pieces. Return to oven for 1 minute. Spread melted chocolate evenly over top of bars. Sprinkle with almonds. Cool in pan on a wire rack.

Use foil to lift uncut bars out of pan. Cut or break into bars.

TO STORE: Layer bars between sheets of waxed paper in an airtight container. Cover and refrigerate for up to 3 days or freeze for up to 3 months.

Dark Chocolate Brownies

Dark Chocolate Brownies

Rich and decadent brownies don't get any better! For special get-togethers, offer these with assorted flavors of ice creams and toppers.

- 14 ounces unsweetened chocolate, coarsely chopped
- 1½ cups butter
- ½ cup water
- 2 cups granulated sugar
- 1½ cups packed brown sugar
- 4 eggs
- 2 teaspoons vanilla
- 2⅔ cups all-purpose flour
- ¼ teaspoon salt
- ¼ teaspoon ground cinnamon
  Vanilla or coffee ice cream (optional)
  Chocolate-flavor syrup (optional)

Preheat oven to 350°F. Lightly grease bottom of a 13×9×2-inch baking pan; set aside.

In a saucepan combine chocolate, butter, and water; cook and stir over low heat until chocolate is melted.

Transfer to a large mixing bowl. Add granulated sugar and brown sugar to the chocolate mixture; beat with an electric mixer on low to medium speed until combined. Add eggs and vanilla; beat on medium speed for 2 minutes. Add flour, salt, and cinnamon; beat on low speed until combined. Spread batter in prepared baking pan.

Bake about 25 minutes or until a wooden toothpick inserted near center comes out clean. Cool in pan on a wire rack about 30 minutes or until brownies hold a cut edge. Cut into bars.

If desired, top each brownie with a scoop of ice cream and drizzle with chocolate syrup.

TO STORE: Layer bars between sheets of waxed paper in an airtight container. Cover and store at room temperature for up to 3 days or freeze for up to 3 months.

Loaded
Chocolate Cookies

Loaded Chocolate Cookies

Three varieties of chocolate take these cookies over the top.

⅔ cup butter, softened
⅔ cup shortening
1 cup granulated sugar
1 cup packed brown sugar
1 teaspoon baking soda
½ teaspoon salt
2 eggs
2 teaspoons vanilla
⅓ cup unsweetened cocoa powder
3 cups all-purpose flour
1½ cups semisweet chocolate pieces
1 cup coarsely chopped macadamia nuts
½ cup milk chocolate pieces

Preheat oven to 375°F. In an extra-large mixing bowl beat butter and shortening with an electric mixer on medium to high speed for 30 seconds. Add the granulated sugar, brown sugar, baking soda, and salt. Beat until mixture is combined, scraping sides of bowl occasionally. Beat in the eggs and vanilla. Beat in the cocoa powder. Beat in as much of the flour as you can with the mixer. Stir in any remaining flour. Stir in semisweet chocolate pieces, macadamia nuts, and milk chocolate pieces.

Using a ¼-cup measure, drop dough about 4 inches apart onto ungreased cookie sheets. If desired, flatten dough mounds to circles about ¾ inch thick. Bake for 12 to 14 minutes or until edges are set. Cool on cookie sheet on wire rack for 2 minutes. Transfer cookies to wire rack to cool. Makes 24 cookies.

TO STORE: Layer cookies between sheets of waxed paper in an airtight container. Cover and store at room temperature for up to 3 days or freeze for up to 3 months.

Peanut Butter-Chocolate Squares

Guests will revel in the dynamic duo of chocolate and peanut butter. When serving the dessert, use a hot knife to make clean cuts in the squares.

1 9-ounce package chocolate wafer cookies, finely crushed
½ cup packed brown sugar
¼ teaspoon salt
½ cup butter, melted
1 teaspoon vanilla
1 8-ounce package cream cheese, softened
1 cup peanut butter
1 cup milk
2 4-serving-size packages French vanilla instant pudding and pie filling mix
5 cups frozen whipped dessert topping, thawed
1 cup dry-roasted peanuts, coarsely chopped
1 7-ounce tub dipping chocolate*
  Miniature chocolate-covered peanut butter cups (optional)
  Chopped dry-roasted peanuts (optional)

Preheat oven to 325°F. In a medium bowl stir together crushed cookies, brown sugar, and salt. Add melted butter and vanilla; stir until mixture is evenly moist.

For crust, press cookie mixture firmly and evenly onto bottom of a 3-quart rectangular baking dish. Bake for 8 to 10 minutes or until crust is firm. Cool in dish on a wire rack.

In a large mixing bowl beat cream cheese and peanut butter with an electric mixer on medium to high speed until light and fluffy, scraping bowl occasionally. Add milk and pudding mixes; beat for 3 minutes. Fold in 2 cups of the whipped topping and the 1 cup peanuts. Spoon peanut butter mixture evenly over crust; spread evenly. Cover and chill for at least 1 hour.

Peanut Butter-Chocolate Squares

In a microwave melt dipping chocolate according to package directions. Cool slightly. In a medium bowl whisk together melted dipping chocolate and the remaining 3 cups whipped topping until well combined.

Spread chocolate mixture evenly over the peanut butter layer. Cover and chill for at least 4 hours or overnight. If desired, garnish each serving with a peanut butter cup and/or peanuts. Cut into squares. Makes 20 to 24 servings.

*TEST KITCHEN TIP: Look for dipping chocolate in the baking aisle of supermarkets.

Raspberry French
Silk Bars

Raspberry French Silk Bars

Chocolate Crumb Crust
1 cup whipping cream
½ cup chopped semisweet chocolate (3 ounces)
½ cup chopped bittersweet chocolate (3 ounces)
⅓ cup sugar
⅓ cup butter
2 egg yolks, beaten
3 tablespoons crème de cacao or whipping cream
½ cup raspberry preserves or seedless raspberry jam
Raspberry Ganache
Fresh raspberries (optional)

Preheat oven to 375°F. Line a 13×9×2-inch baking pan with foil, extending the foil over the edges of the pan. Press Chocolate Crumb Crust onto the bottom and slightly up the sides of the prepared pan. Bake for about 10 minutes or until crust is set. Cool completely in pan on a wire rack. Set aside.

Meanwhile, for filling, in a heavy medium saucepan combine whipping cream, chocolates, sugar, and butter. Cook and stir over low heat for about 10 minutes or until chocolates are melted and smooth. Remove from heat. Gradually stir half the hot mixture into beaten egg yolks. Add egg yolk mixture to chocolate mixture in saucepan. Cook and stir over medium-low heat about 5 minutes or until mixture is slightly thickened and bubbly.

Remove from heat. (Mixture may appear slightly curdled.) Stir in the crème de cacao. Place the saucepan in a bowl of ice water. Stir occasionally for about 20 minutes or until the mixture stiffens and becomes hard to stir. Transfer the filling to a medium mixing bowl.

Spread raspberry preserves over cooled Chocolate Crumb Crust.

Caramel Sandwich Cookies

Beat filling with an electric mixer on medium to high speed for 2 to 3 minutes or until light and fluffy. Spread filling over preserves. Cover and chill for
1 to 2 hours or until firm. Prepare Raspberry Ganache.

Remove bars from refrigerator. Spoon Raspberry Ganache over top, gently spreading evenly. Cover and chill for 1 to 2 hours more or until firm. Using the edges of the foil, lift the uncut bars out of the pan. Cut into bars. If desired, garnish with fresh raspberries. Makes 32 bars.

CHOCOLATE CRUMB CRUST: In a medium bowl combine 2 cups finely crushed chocolate wafers, ¼ cup all-purpose flour, and 2 tablespoons granulated sugar. Add ½ cup melted butter and stir until well combined.

RASPBERRY GANACHE: In a large glass measuring cup combine 1 cup chopped semisweet chocolate or chocolate pieces, ⅓ cup whipping cream, and 1 tablespoon seedless raspberry jam. Microwave on 100-percent power (high) for about 1 minute or until chocolate is melted, stirring every 30 seconds. Let stand about 1 hour or until slightly thickened.

Caramel Sandwich Cookies

⅔ cup broken pecans
½ cup sugar
¼ teaspoon salt
1 cup unsalted butter, slightly softened and cut up
2 teaspoons vanilla
2 cups all-purpose flour
Caramel Filling
6 ounces white baking chocolate with cocoa butter or white baking pieces

In a food processor combine pecans, sugar, and salt. Cover and process until nuts are finely ground. Add butter and vanilla. Cover and process until butter is smooth. Add flour; cover and process until a soft dough starts to form around the blade. Transfer dough to a medium bowl; knead gently until smooth.

Shape dough into a 12-inch roll. Wrap in plastic wrap or waxed paper. Chill for about 2 hours or until firm enough to slice.

Preheat oven to 350°F. Cut roll into scant ¼-inch slices. Place about 1 inch apart on an ungreased cookie sheet. Bake for 10 to 12 minutes or until edges are golden brown. Cool on cookie sheet for 1 to 2 minutes. Transfer to a wire rack; cool.

Spread 1 rounded teaspoon Caramel Filling on bottoms of half the cookies. Top with the remaining cookies, bottom sides down.

Melt white chocolate according to package directions. Dip one end of each cookie into melted chocolate. Let stand on waxed paper until set. Makes about 25 sandwich cookies.

CARAMEL FILLING: In a small saucepan combine 24 vanilla caramels and ¼ cup whipping cream. Cook and stir over low heat just until melted.

Cute Quackers ▶

Decorate yellow-frosted cupcakes with a flock of springtime chicks. To make the head, cut a slit in a large yellow gumdrop for the beak. Cut a triangular slice from a small orange gumdrop and press it into the slit for the beak. Use a toothpick to indent eye areas and press in a small candy decorating sprinkle for each eye. For wings, cut a large yellow gumdrop in half and shape points. Press the pieces into the frosting.

Easy Does It
Top It Off

◀ Polka Dot Delight

Mint and chocolate make a tasty pair. Poke the points of mints into a mini cake, allowing the nonpareil bottoms to dot the cake frosting.

Flower Power

Individually packaged cakes get a major facelift with the addition of fresh flowers. Take the wrapper off the cake. Cut a piece of cellophane or plastic wrap slightly larger than its top. Gently lay it on top and press a short-clipped stem into the center of the cake.

Blooming Beauties

Plant pretty edible pokes into green-frosted cupcakes. Use toothpicks to skewer jellied sugared candies, such as spearmint leaves, candy rings, and gum drops.

Grand Stand

Present a mini cupcake on an ice cream cone topped with a flattened cupcake liner. If you like ice cream with your treat, fill the cone before placing the cupcake.

SALUTE SUMMER

Embrace sunshine and carefree days with summer-style projects you'll be proud to share with family and friends.

Amazing Vase

Bring fresh-cut flowers inside to vases that sing with character. Once clear and simple, these now-elegant flower holders shine all summer long.

Glass on Glass

■ Flat decorative marbles add dimension, color, and pattern to a large round vase. Use a low-temp glue gun to attach the small marbles, filling in open areas with larger pieces.

A

B

C

Fresh Meets Frosted

■ Graphic etched patterns create a soft backdrop for flowers. Brush on etching cream in random designs or use one of these tape methods.

What You'll Need...

- ☐ masking tape
- ☐ smooth clear glass vase or rose bowl
- ☐ scissors
- ☐ glass etching cream

1 **To make a multistripe vase,** pull down tape strips from the top of the vase as shown in Photo A.

2 **Cut off the tape** at random lengths as shown in Photo B. Cover the vase with tape, overlapping at the top, if needed so tape lines are vertical.

3 **Brush etching cream** on the untaped areas of the vase, as shown in Photo C, following the manufacturer's instructions. Rinse off the etching cream as directed and remove the tape.

4 **To make a single horizontal stripe** rose bowl, tear a narrow strip of masking tape and press it around the center of the bowl. Apply etching cream as in Step 3.

Plastic Wrap

■ Inexpensive plastic place mats come in endless color combinations and patterns. Choose an oval one and wrap it around a vase, using double-sided tape or hot glue to adhere the ends together. If you use tape, you can replace the place mat with every season.

Scrunch and Crunch

■ Turn to paper napkins to create a textural coating to blanket a smooth vase. Check party and dollar stores to find colors that coordinate with your decorating scheme.

What You'll Need...

- [ ] patterned paper napkins
- [ ] scissors
- [ ] decoupage medium
- [ ] smooth clear glass vase
- [ ] paintbrush

1 Cut off folds of several paper napkins; peel away the backing paper from the top layer as shown in Photo A.

2 Scrunch up each colored paper piece as shown in Photo B.

3 Working in small sections, brush decoupage medium onto the vase as shown in Photo C and press scrunched paper onto wet decoupage medium as shown in Photo D.

4 Gently brush more decoupage medium on the placed paper piece as shown in Photo E.

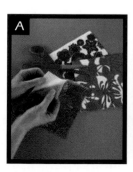

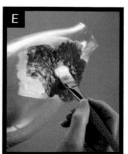

Grand Central

■ Let your garden inspire the colors and arrangement on a green-laden table. Combine potted plants with other symbols of nature and the scene works as beautifully as it does by the fence.

Blooms & Butterflies

Clever and fresh, this warm-weather sensation pulls out all the stops. From bird nests to flowerpots and white picket fences to butterflies, you'll feel like you're in a lovely wildflower meadow when you sit down at this table saturated with summer.

Sweet Setting

■ This place setting is so welcoming, guests will feel extra special when the dinner bell rings. Green paper plates help to marry the dishes with the rest of the table. For a theme-fitting napkin ring, start with a small grapevine wreath. Tie it with a loose ribbon, wire on an artificial bird, and tuck in a tiny flower sprig.

Flea Market Find

■ An old birdcage, spray painted with a crisp coat of white, adds a nice touch to this tabletop sanctuary. Look for old cages at flea markets, garage sales, and in antiques stores. Or check crafts and home decor shops for new finds.

Guest Nest

■ A crafts store nest creates a bowl to hold a few take-home goodies. To line the nest, dye a coffee filter using food coloring. To make the edible eggs, melt white chocolate as directed. When soft, mix in a drop of blue food coloring. Put on heat-resistant gloves. While soft, use a tableknife to press warmed chocolate into the halves of mini Easter eggs. Press halves together and chill in refrigerator.

White-Washed Place Mat

■ Natural bamboo gets a layer of shabby chic when brushed with a light coat of white craft paint. The trick to this technique is to use a lightly loaded brush to give the mat a time-worn appearance.

Flight Pattern

■ Just like nature, these scrapbook paper butterflies have
showy patterned wings. Use the patterns on page 157
as inspiration for cutting the shapes, then layer a pair of
wings or let them fly solo. The body, crafted from a thin
chenille stem, wraps around the wing centers. Twist the
chenille stems together to secure, then curve antennae
ends. To attach the butterflies to a twig wreath, simply
slip the twig through backs of the chenille stems.

Burst of Summer

■ This bright display is sure to set a happy mood. Arrange fresh-cut flowers in a watering can (lined if not watertight). Tie a ribbon bow to the handle and perch a couple of wired butterflies to look as though they too are enjoying the view.

Desk Doodads for Dad

Delight Dad this Father's Day with handsome wood desk accessories he'll be proud to use.

Handsome Holder

■ A recycled can makes it easy to create a round pencil holder from craft sticks. Hot-glue the sticks around the outside of the can, aligning at the bottom. Wrap the center of the holder with a wide ribbon and tack down the ends with hot glue.

No Ordinary Organizer

■ Wood boxes can be found in all shapes and sizes in crafts stores. To make them desk worthy, dress up the lid with striking papers. Cut shapes that correspond with the lid in two different sizes. Use decoupage medium to adhere the layered papers to the center of the lid. Mark the center of the lid and drill a hole in it. Attach a drawer-pull handle, using washer spacers underneath if needed.

Picture Pals

These photo holders are so easy to make, even the kids can join in the assembly line. Using a wood toy wheel as the base, press the dowel end of a small wood finial into the opening in the wheel, securing with hot glue if necessary. Poke a hole in the top of the finial using an ice pick or awl. In a well-ventilated work area, spray the wood pieces with clear acrylic. Form a piece of heavy craft wire into a spiral with a 1-inch straight end. Insert the wire into the top of the finial, securing with hot-glue.

Stars and Stripes

Down-Home Fare

■ Denim-color sap buckets and bandana napkins are pure Americana touches on a casual table dressed in blue. Painted with red stripes, the rabbit weather vane jumps out as a folk-art centerpiece.

Sandy Stripes

■ Undulating bands of sand subtly echo the theme of the porch. Pour alternating layers of white and red sand into a hurricane vase or other clear glass container, then insert a pillar candle.

Forever

Strike an all-American pose outdoors with everyday items and collectibles.

American Made

■ Layered in red, white, and blue, any outdoor space becomes patriotic. Set the scene by hanging a flag (hang the union-blue field at the top left as it is viewed from the street or yard). Striped fabric tied to the railing with heavy blue yarn imitates classic bunting.

Star-Struck Wreath

■ Laced with striped ribbon, this tin star is glory bound. Attach a star to a preserved boxwood wreath for a summery green backdrop, or use a straw or grapevine wreath.

Flag-Waving Bouquet

■ Grouped in a vase, miniature flags make a long-lasting centerpiece that easily reinforces a stars-and-stripes scheme. Place the flags in a vintage floral frog or other gridded vessel for a free-flowing look.

Light Show

■ Day or night, paper lanterns provide a star-spangled view. String ready-made lanterns from a multi-socket lantern cord. Hang from cup hooks.

Frames to Love

Bridal White

■ This stunning accent transforms a plain white picture frame in only a couple of minutes. Cut a square of tulle slightly shorter than the frame height. Gather it in the center and secure with a brooch. Hot-glue the decoration to the frame glass, arranging to enhance the photo.

When you need a wedding gift, these photo frames make wonderful vow-day surprises for the bride and groom. Check out flea markets, secondhand shops, department stores, or your own jewelry box to find gem-studded jewelry accents.

Old-Fashioned Elegance

■ Metallic accents add a ritzy touch to an ordinary picture frame. Start by painting a familiar saying or words of wisdom around the frame and let the paint dry. Use hot glue to hold a brooch-embellished tulle bow on one side and a pair of matching earrings arranged together opposite it.

Let each of the kids craft their own party hat. Supply each child with a sheet of school-theme scrapbook paper and show them how to roll it into a cap shape. Help the kids tape the paper together and trim the edge even. Use adhesive letters to deck out the front and have plenty of pom-pom balls on hand for trimming the edge and point. Use crafts glue or hot-glue, depending on the ages of the partygoers.

Easy Does It

A+ Party

You Got Class

When hosting a back-to-school party, this clever place setting more than makes the grade. Layer fun plastic dishes and top with an apple donning a paper leaf message. Tear apart a desk calendar to use as place mats around the table.

An Apple a Day ▶
Give guests a healthy apple snack with a fun message attached. Cut simple leaf shapes from card stock and write a note on the top leaf. Attach the paper accents with a toothpick.

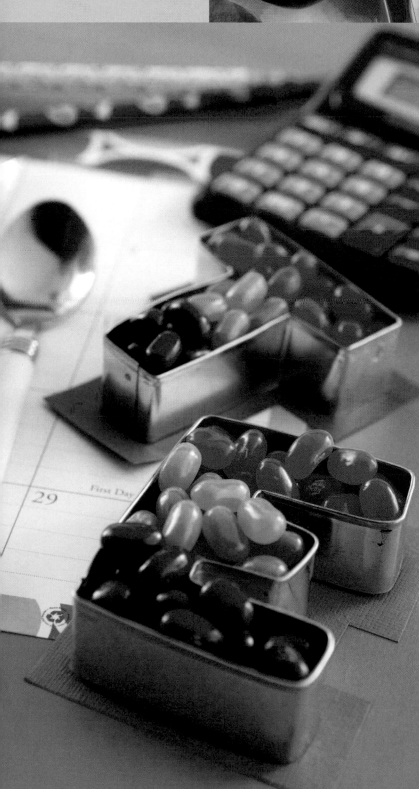

▲ **Fun Stuff**
Kids love to get new school supplies, so these gifts are sure to be a hit. Fill water bottles with pencils and rulers and use adhesive foam letters to add the guest's name. Use foam numbers to add fun detail to mini notebooks too.

◀ **Initially Yours**
Personalize party favors using cookie cutters in guests' initials. Trace onto colored card stock and cut out ¼ inch beyond lines. Use tape to secure the cutter to the paper, running tape from the inside of the cutter onto the paper. Lay the letters flat and fill with small candies.

BOO-TIFY *your* HOME

Be ready when goblins come to call with tasty treats and cleverly concocted decorations strewn about.

Create a Mood

■ Before dinner, let guests mingle around a wickedly indulgent wine and cheese spread, including black fruits, crackers, and breads. Squat Cinderella pumpkins stand in as pedestals for cheese trays. Chalk black labels for cheeses and wine bottles. Let tarnished silver pieces add to the dark ambience; use them as unique perches for small pumpkins. Spray-paint branches white or black and anchor in tall cylindrical vases for eerie accents.

Sophisticated Fright

Throw a grown-up Halloween party this year. Classic dark fiction inspires a wealth of scary—yet intriguing—ideas.

Good Read

■ Draw guests into the party theme with snippets of ghostly tales tucked around the table.

Wrapped Up

■ Create added interest by wrapping pumpkins and gourds with vine, raffia, or straw. Stack the spheres for a dramatic look.

QUOTH THE
RAVEN:
NEVERMORE
NEVERMORE
NEVERMORE
NEVERM

EDGAR ALLAN POE

ILLUSTRATED BY MARK SUMMERS   INTRODUCTION BY NEIL GAIMAN

Complete Tales & Poems

Set the Stage

Greet guests at the door with hints of what's to come.
Write the classic line from Edgar Allan Poe's "The Raven" on
a blackboard or hard black posterboard. Books feature the
celebrated author's tales of terror, setting the tone of the party.
A vintage typewriter puts an exclamation point on the literary
theme.

Decorate the Set

■ Discreetly wired to the chandelier, a raven looms over the dinner party. Stacks of black books become varied-height pedestals for pumpkins and vases of dried flowers

Wrap It Up

■ Send guests home with mini takeout boxes tied with string. Fill each box with fall-motif cookies, one last Poe tale, and chocolates.

The Plot Sweetens

■ After dinner, move the storytelling away from the table with a tantalizing sideboard of dark and decadent sweets. Use a tiered server or stack cake plates on pumpkins to serve black jelly beans, licorice sticks, and wrapped dark chocolates. Scattered dried leaves add a cost-free decorative element.

Turn the Page

■ Make place mats by taping together pages from Poe's books. Layer black dessert plates and napkins on dinnerware. White Baby Boo pumpkins and dried grapevine secure hand-cut place cards lettered with adhesive letters. As the grand finale, include a pressed leaf topped with a pocket-journal gift and a page from a thriller to add fall color.

Seasonal Seating

A rustic chair gets a shot of fall color when topped with a collection of gourds, squash, and pumpkins.

From the Pumpkin Patch

No carving skills required for these showy autumnal arrangements.

Round and About

■ Miniature pumpkins fit snugly between the spokes of an old-style wagon wheel. Lean the wheel against a tree to bring a touch of rustic autumn charm to your yard.

Pumpkin Peddler

■ A vintage bicycle gets its own autumn twist with mini pumpkins tucked into its spokes and a larger pumpkin parked on the seat.

Pumpkins Aplenty

■ To make a pumpkin tree, fill a glass cylinder vase with birdseed and stick in a few sturdy branches. Drill a small hole in the stem of each pumpkin, string fishing line or florist's wire through the hole, and hang.

Living Table Runner

■ Weave double-face ribbon around miniature pumpkins or gourds for a fresh-from-the-pumpkin patch table runner. Top with a bittersweet stem for a blaze of color worthy of the Thanksgiving table. The super-simple presentation also works well on a mantel.

Nature's Finest

■ A pyramid of fall fruits and miniature squash plated on a birch-log pedestal is a simple but beautiful centerpiece. Place a woven charger under the place to marry the elements.

Banner Place Setting

■ Flag guests down for dinner with place cards made from ribbon markers skewered into plump gourds.

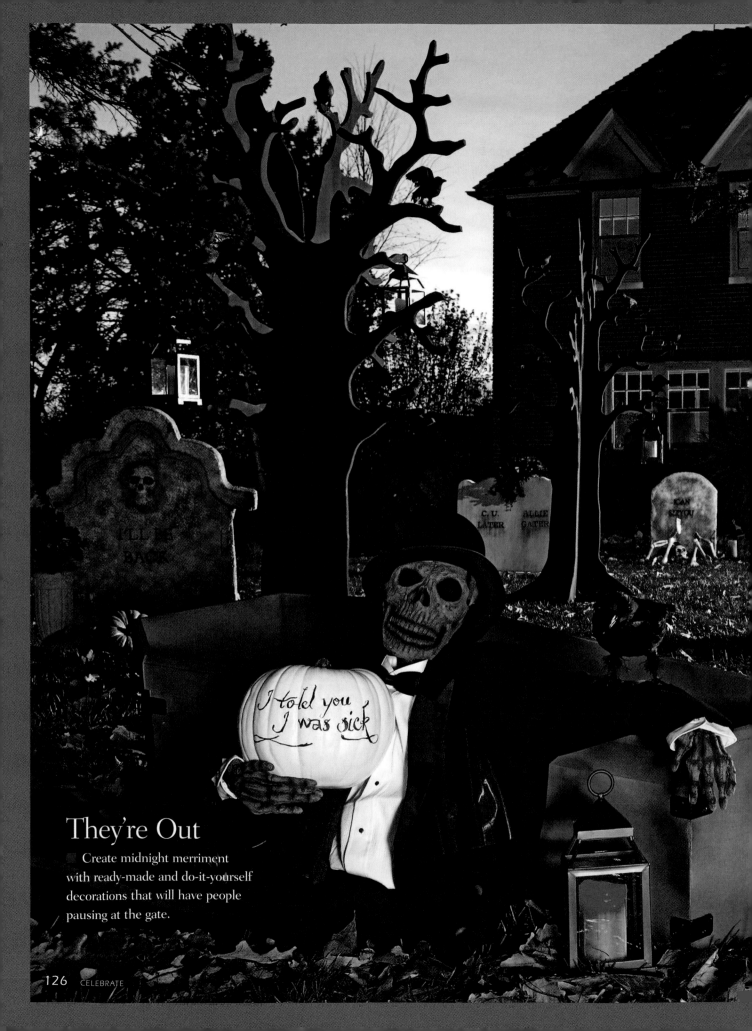

They're Out

Create midnight merriment with ready-made and do-it-yourself decorations that will have people pausing at the gate.

Open
at
MIDNIGHT

714

VACANCY

Fashion a fiendishly funny family plot to welcome guests to your own weird world.

Creeping Up Outside

Sinister Silhouettes

■ No spooky cemetery would be complete without scraggly trees silhouetted against the night sky and decked with lanterns and crows, which lend an eerie aura to the gravesite. The dimensional 8-foot-tall trees, crafted from spray-painted plywood, feature slot joinery so they stand alone. Cut out two 8-foot-high trees with trunks approximately 1 foot wide using the photo for pattern ideas. On one tree piece, cut a 3-foot-long slit up the center of the trunk from the bottom. On the remaining piece, cut a slit down the center of the trunk, stopping 3 feet from the bottom. Spray-paint black, let dry, and connect the two pieces by sliding the bottom-slit tree over the top-slit tree.

Eerie Escape

■ It looks like one fellow has nearly escaped the bonds of the world beyond. To create this illusion, disassemble a fake skeleton and arrange the arms, legs, and head in a petrifying pose. To give the tombstone an aged look, randomly spray on a light coat of green paint.

I told you
I was sick

Dapper Dead

With a jaunty tip of his top hat and a ghoulish grin, this fellow's ready to join the festivities. Browse secondhand clothing stores for new or vintage finery to dress skeleton characters in style.

Perfect Perch

■ This fellow is wearing a coat of realistic-looking spray-on stone paint to match his monument.

Host with the Most

■ Every haunted gathering needs a macabre master for a host. This dapper gent sports the latest in formal fashion.

Portentous Promise

■ A ghoul peers from this tombstone, with its message making a bone-chilling prediction. To create the look, cut a hole through a foam tombstone, insert a plastic skeleton head, and camouflage edges with spackling.

Spooky Store Hours

■ Merry mayhem is the order of the evening and midnight is the magic hour. A foam cutter tool's warm blade easily cuts cracks and relief letters.

Space Available

■ It pays to advertise and this stone declares there's always room for one more to join the motley band below. A rotary crafts tool easily carves the realistic lettering and arrow. And a wood file rounds the edges to simulate the look of weathered stone.

What You'll Need...

- [ ] 2-inch-thick, 24x36-inch foam sheets
- [ ] foam saw
- [ ] wood file
- [ ] foam cutter, such as Styro Wonder Cutter Plus
- [ ] repositionable spray adhesive
- [ ] rotary carving tool
- [ ] household trim brush
- [ ] acrylic crafts paints in black, gray, brown, copper, white, and other colors as desired
- [ ] foam trim roller

1 To make a tombstone, draw the desired shape onto foam sheet, and cut out. Use a wood file to round all edges and create a timeworn look.

2 To make cracks, cut away a portion with the cutter and score an indentation where the cracks end.

3 For lettering, choose a font, type in desired words, and print out in size to fit tombstone. Cut words apart and apply to the tombstone with repositionable spray adhesive. Carve out the letters, using either a rotary tool with a round chuck or the cutter.

4 To create the basic stone look, use the household trim brush and push black paint into all carved areas and cracks. Let dry. Use a foam trim roller to base-coat the tombstone with dark gray. Paint as desired.

Tongue-in-Cheek Tombstone

■ With a touch of cheeky humor, Mr. Later and Ms. Gater eagerly await their reunion. Meanwhile, their headstone, paint-streaked for an aged look, appears to have been decorated decades ago, with its bouquet of flowers spray-painted to look as if it's seen better days.

Groovy Graveyard

Create a spine-tingling scene sure to entertain guests and passersby with eerie realism. Use slabs of foam, paint, and readily available props to assemble a family plot full of fun.

R I P

DM BONES

VACANCY

Too Soon To Go

Quick Cups

Cupcake liners donning Halloween motifs work well to hold a small sampling of treats. Hot-glue liners to layered circles cut from scrapbook papers.

Haunting Handouts

Surprise trick-or-treaters with individually wrapped treats that add festive flair to beggars' night.

Recycled Wrappers

■ From pumpkin seeds to costumes and candy, you may be surprised at how you can make the most of your Halloween product packaging. Use the timely designs to wrap candy bars for trick-or-treaters.

Message Jars

■ Etching cream gives glass jars a cloudy coat. Follow the manufacturer's directions for etching, rinsing off, and drying. Add a sticker letter message or word on the jar and tie ribbons around the jar necks.

A Cutter Above

■ Prepainted cookie cutters tout Halloween silhouettes. Trace around a cutter on card stock and trim slightly outside drawn line. Hot-glue bottom of cookie cutter to paper cutout. Trim edge of paper with metallic silver chenille stem, hot-glued in place. Fill with candies. If transporting, slip treat into a cellophane candy bag and seal closed.

Eye've Got It

■ Pull-apart ornaments can hold a handful of Halloween candy. To make them appear as eyeballs, in a well-ventilated area, spray-paint each half white and let dry. Use the patterns on page 158 to cut two circles, each from a card stock square larger than ornament. Using the large circle cutout, place on one side of ornament and spray-paint green. Let dry and lightly mist edge with black spray paint; let dry and remove paper pattern. Place small circle cutout on center of spray-painted green circle, paint black, and let dry. To display, connect the halves and hang from chenille stem hangers on a tree branch, securely "planted" in cement in a large flowerpot.

Train of Terror

Set the stage for a hauntingly fun Halloween get-together with a tabletop train wreck that's full of tricks and treats.

Ghost Town

Create a looming Halloween landscape around which to gather for eerie eats. Layered batik and gauze fabrics blanket the table as a skeleton propped atop a tiered tray beckons guests to take a seat.

Graveyard Shift

■ A skeleton crew adds ghastly character to the scene. Shape bones and oval heads from white oven-bake clay. To add facial details, poke the ovals with a pencil. Bake the clay according to manufacturer's directions and let cool.

Rail Rider

■ Arrange toy train cars along disjointed tracks with a smattering of clay bones strewn about.

Tabletop Trees

■ Miniature leafless trees are easy to craft. For each stark tree, hot-glue a large wood bead to a square of cardboard. Glue a twig inside the bead and spray paint black to present an eerie silhouette.

Under Wraps

■ Add mummy appeal to a fresh pear, perfectly ready for devouring. Wrap pear with a length of gauze bandage, secured in place by pulling ends over the stem.

Pumpkin Panache

Glued, painted, or carved, these pumpkins add a touch of class to Halloween decorating.

Boo-Rah!

Ready to raise some Halloween hackles? With a jarful of black buttons and a bottle of glue, you can give any pumpkin a ghostly shout.

Faux Candy Corn

■ Yellow and white spray paint coat pumpkins to resemble colossal candy corn. Before painting, wrap stems with low-tack masking tape. Paint a yellow stripe around the bottom and the top tip white. Remove the tape.

Glowing Gourds

■ Turn a collection of squatty gourds into a goofy troupe of grinning jack-o'-lanterns for your doorstep. Don't worry about your carving skills here – their crooked smiles and mesmerizing eyes are all about the charm of imperfection.

Pattern Play

■ Give pumpkins delicate patterns with paint and stencils made from paper doilies. Cut out the center of the doily and spray the back with repositionable adhesive; let dry. Place doily ring on pumpkin and press to secure, cutting slits if necessary to fit. Using a stencil brush and a small amount of craft paint, dab paint into openings. Allow paint to dry slightly, then carefully remove doily.

Pumpkin Pots

■ Pot bright fall mums in a matched set of pumpkins. Choose flowers in 4- or 6-inch pots, carve openings in the tops of the pumpkins, and slip the pots in.

Letter-Perfect

■ Select a font you like on a computer. Enlarge the letter to fit the pumpkin and print it out. Transfer the letter to the pumpkin. Using a knife or carving tools, cut out the openings.

Tricks
with Treats

Clever creativity comes with monstrously good Halloween treats and sweets that are ready to thrill and be savored.

Jack-o'-Lantern Cheese Ball

■ Make your favorite cream cheese ball recipe. Roll ball in crushed nacho-cheese flavor snack chips. Place ball on a kale-lined platter. Cut pitted ripe olives into triangle-shaped pieces. Press olive pieces into ball, making eyes and a mouth (you may need to remove chips from those areas to help them stick). Place a dill pickle half on top for a stem.

Batty Bites

For a large bat, cut a chocolate-flavor breakfast pastry in half diagonally. For a small bat, cut a chocolate-flavor breakfast pastry in half diagonally and then in half again, making four triangles.

To make a bat, carefully dip one side of two pastry triangles into melted semisweet chocolate. Place triangles, chocolate sides up, on a baking sheet lined with waxed paper. Embellish triangle wings with decorative sprinkles.

Dip a chocolate cream-filled sandwich cookie (large for a large bat and miniature for a small bat) into melted chocolate. Place a cookie body on top of the triangle wings. Add eyes of almonds, sunflower kernels, and/or pumpkin seeds. For the almond eyes, use miniature chocolate pieces as pupils. Chill until chocolate is set.

Cockeyed Cuckoos

■ For each sandwich, spoon two hot marinara-sauced meatballs on a split and toasted roll. Roll two small pieces of cream cheese into balls.

■ Gently push a cream cheese ball in each meatball, making an eye. Cut pitted ripe olives into small pieces; press on each cream cheese ball as a pupils. Cut orange and/or yellow sweet peppers in pieces; arrange on meatballs as beaks and eyebrows. Arrange julienne carrots and/or chives on sandwiches to resemble feathers.

Spooky Stew

Spoon your favorite hot stew into individual serving dishes, filling each about two-thirds full. Using a pastry bag fitted with a large plain round tip, pipe hot mashed potatoes into a ghost shape on top of each. Use capers for ghost eyes. Sprinkle shredded cheddar cheese around the base of each ghost.

The Tombstone Trio

■ For each skeleton, cut a large marshmallow in half, forming two rounds. Dip marshmallow rounds and some thick pretzel stick pieces into melted white baking chocolate; place on a baking sheet lined with waxed paper. Chill until set.

■ Using a pastry bag fitted with a small round tip, pipe chocolate frosting onto marshmallow halves to make skeleton faces. Pipe a little frosting on a chocolate graham cracker and attach a marshmallow skeleton head. Pipe a little frosting lengthwise onto the undersides of coated pretzel pieces, attaching them to the graham crackers to create a skeleton body. Use some melted white baking chocolate to pipe ribs onto the skeleton over the spine.

■ Line a serving platter with green tinted coconut "grass." Sprinkle on crushed chocolate graham crackers as "soil." Stick the remaining marshmallow halves partly underneath the skeleton-topped graham crackers to prop them up; place on "ground." Using chocolate frosting, decorate a chocolate-filled butter cookie as a tombstone. Stick a cookie into each marshmallow half, positioning it as a tombstone.

"Hairry" the Scary Spider

☐ Prepare and bake one 1-layer cake mix according to package directions, except pour batter into a greased and floured 1½-quart glass mixing bowl. Bake for 35 to 40 minutes or until a toothpick inserted near center comes out clean. Let cake stand at room temperature for 5 minutes.

Remove cake from bowl and cool completely, top side down, on a wire rack.

☐ Cut 8 cream-filled wafer cookies in half at a slight angle. Dip the angled ends of each cookie into some melted semisweet chocolate;

place the two dipped ends together on the baking sheet lined with waxed paper to form a leg. Chill until chocolate is set.

☐ Frost rounded surface of cake with chocolate frosting. Add white licorice pastel candies to make a mouth. Place rounded pastel wafer candies as eyes. Use frosting to stick on candy-coated milk chocolate pieces as pupils. Cut two corners from red licorice candy; use pointy corners as fangs. Top cake with curly grated milk chocolate. Insert cookie legs into each side of cake.

Paper layers in Halloween colors make an interesting invitation. End with die-cut black paper for the top layer, enhancing it with press-on gems. Write party information on white paper, glue it to the back of the decorative side, and trim with more gems.

Easy Does It
Eerie Invitations

◀ **Party Crower**

This dimensional invitation sets the tone with major Halloween spirit. Wire an artificial bird to layered squares of scrapbook paper, one printed with the words, "Unroll the Scroll … If You Dare." Craft a miniature hat for the black bird with a paper scrap and trim with metallic chenille stem and a pom-pom. Hot-glue it in place. Print the party information and roll it scroll form. Wrap the paper with a short length of chenille stem.

Clever Disguise
Trace an eye mask shape onto orange paper and trim out using decorative-edge scissors. Write party information on the orange paper, leaving left edge unprinted. Attach the mask to the paper using a gem brad. Enhance the mask using more gem brads and stickers.

Boldly Stated
1-inch strips of glitter paper in orange, silver, and black make a vivid card base. Use glue stick to attach the strips to a black note card as shown. Adhesive letters complete the Halloween message.

Chain of Events
Metal-edge tags, available in scrapbook and office supply stores, are just the right size to write a party detail on each one. Cover the backs with seasonal scrapbook paper cut to size and adhere with glue stick. Connect the tags with ball chain.

Patterns

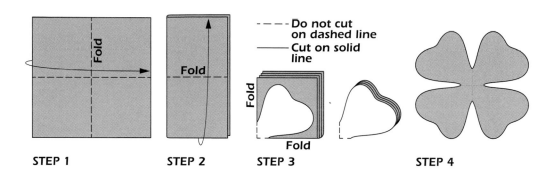

STEP 1   STEP 2   STEP 3   STEP 4

Fold

Fold

Fold

Fold

- - - Do not cut
on dashed line
——— Cut on solid
line

LUCK OF THE IRISH
page 22
Full-Size Pattern

LUCK OF THE IRISH
page 22
Full-Size Pattern

LUCK OF THE IRISH
page 22
Full-Size Pattern

LUCK OF
THE IRISH
page 22
Full-Size Pattern

page 22
Full-Size
Pattern

COZY COMFORT STITCHES
page 14-17

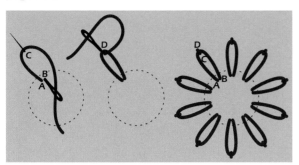

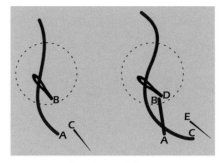

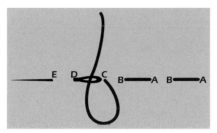

Lazy Daisy Stitch

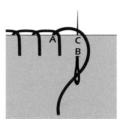

Straight Stitch

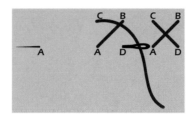

Running Stitch

Cross-Stitch

Blanket Stitch

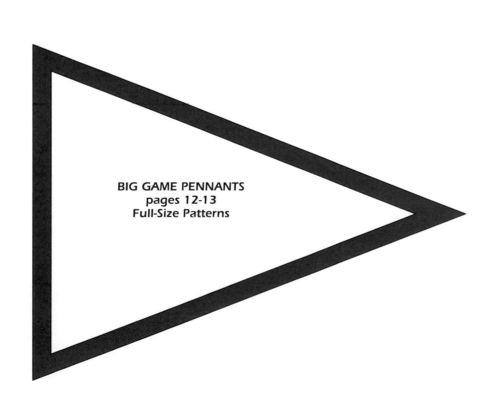

BIG GAME PENNANTS
pages 12-13
Full-Size Patterns

Patterns *continued*

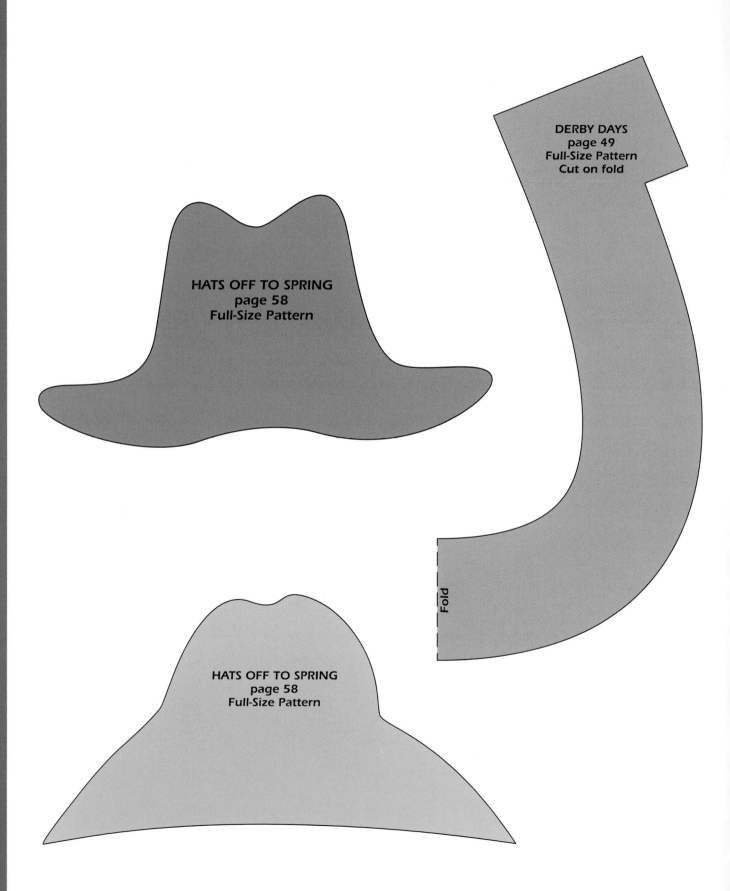

HATS OFF TO SPRING
page 58
Full-Size Pattern

DERBY DAYS
page 49
Full-Size Pattern
Cut on fold

Fold

HATS OFF TO SPRING
page 58
Full-Size Pattern

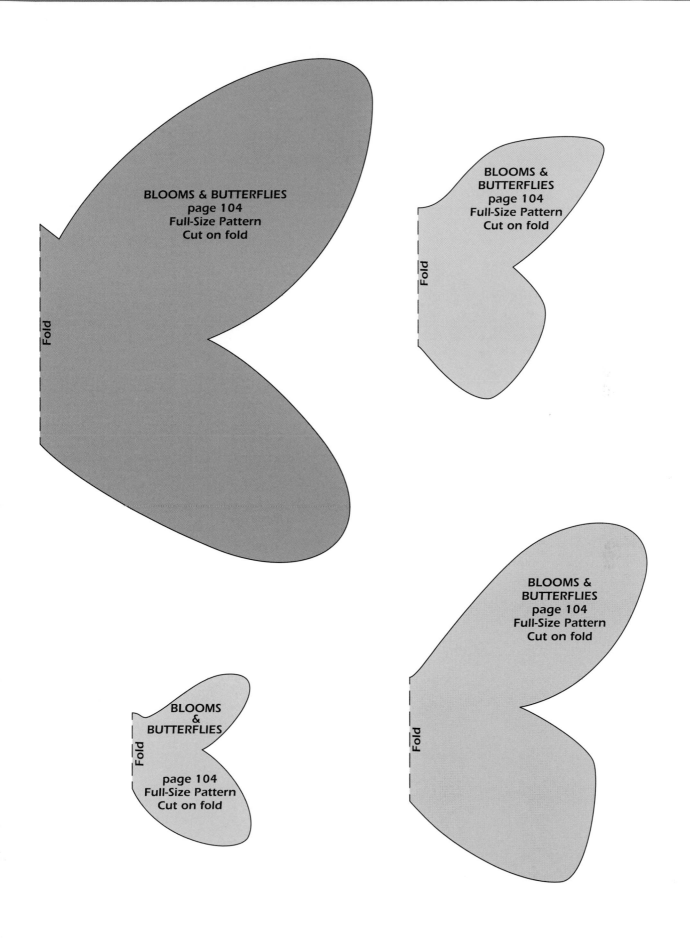

BLOOMS & BUTTERFLIES
page 104
Full-Size Pattern
Cut on fold

Fold

BLOOMS &
BUTTERFLIES
page 104
Full-Size Pattern
Cut on fold

Fold

BLOOMS
&
BUTTERFLIES

Fold

page 104
Full-Size Pattern
Cut on fold

BLOOMS &
BUTTERFLIES
page 104
Full-Size Pattern
Cut on fold

Fold

Patterns *continued*

HALLOWEEN HANDOUT
pages 136-137
Enlarge 120%

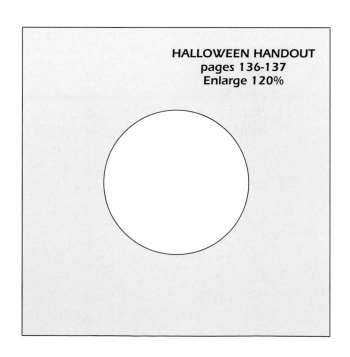

HALLOWEEN HANDOUT
pages 136-137
Enlarge 120%

Index

Index *continued*

credits

PHOTO STYLING
Sue Banker and Cathy Brett

PHOTOGRAPHY
Jay Wilde